Miriam B. Loo's Family Favorites Cookbook

Designed by Linda K. Powell

This book is dedicated to the people who prompted me to share my favorite recipes – the many lovely friends of Current, Inc., who have brightened my days by exchanging recipes with me; the people at Current who have encouraged me to write this cookbook; and, most of all, my husband and sons who never fail to ask, "What's cookin'?", when they see me in the kitchen.

CONTENTS

Dear Friend,

For many years now, it has been a privilege and a pleasure of mine to become acquainted with thousands of women across the country through Current, Inc. I have always considered Current customers to be special friends of mine ... and have been delighted to have the opportunity not only to provide them with Current products, but also to have shared recipes and personal "family" news with them over the years.

It is with particular pleasure, then, that I have written this cookbook to share with you. I have been an avid cook for as long as I can remember, and I love to exchange recipes and share our favorites with friends.

The recipes here are all tried-and-true Loo family favorites. Many are Scandinavian specialties which have been enjoyed in our family for generations. The cookbook has been arranged in sections according to the annual holidays our entire family gathers to celebrate. Of course, good, home-cooked dishes have been a central element of these gatherings ... and I hope these recipes will bring you and your family as much dining pleasure — and leave you with as many warm memories — as they have ours.

Sincerely,

Miriam B. Loo

Miriam B. Loo

Spring

GRANDMA LOBECK'S SPICE CAKE

"moist and spicy . . . so good with Quick Caramel Frosting"

2 cups flour
1 tsp. baking powder
1 tsp. soda
1 tsp. cinnamon
½ tsp. allspice
½ tsp. ground cloves
1½ cups sugar

½ cup shortening
3 eggs
1 tsp. vanilla
1 cup buttermilk or
   sour milk
½ cup raisins
1 cup chopped nuts

Blend together the flour, baking powder, soda and spices. Combine raisins and nuts with 2 tbsp. of the dry ingredients; set aside. Gradually add sugar to shortening in large mixing bowl; cream until light and fluffy. Add eggs, one at a time, beating well after each. Add vanilla to buttermilk. At low speed, add dry ingredients alternately with buttermilk, beginning and ending with dry ingredients. Blend well after each addition. Stir in floured raisins and nuts. Pour batter into greased and lightly floured 13x9-inch pan. Bake at 350° for 35 to 40 min. or until wooden pick inserted in center comes out clean.

Makes 13x9-inch cake

*Altitude Changes: Follow above recipe for Grandma Lobeck's Spice Cake with the following changes:

	3,000 ft.	**5,000 ft.**	**7,000 ft.**
Baking Powder	scant tsp. (⅞) tsp.)	¾ tsp.	¾ tsp.
Sugar	1 cup + 6½ tbsp.	1⅓ cup	1 cup + 3½ tbsp.
Buttermilk or Sour Milk	1 cup + 1 tbsp.	1 cup + 3 tbsp.	1¼ cup

A 10-15 degree increase in baking temperature may give better results. Bake for 30 to 35 min. until cake tests done.

QUICK CARAMEL FROSTING

"rich flavor . . . creamy texture"

⅓ cup butter or margarine
1 cup firmly packed brown sugar
⅛ tsp. salt

¼ cup milk
½ tsp. vanilla
1½ cups confectioners' sugar

Melt butter in saucepan; add brown sugar and cook over low heat 2 min., stirring constantly. Add salt and milk and continue stirring until mixture comes to a boil. Boil 3 min.; remove from heat and cool. Add vanilla; blend well. Gradually beat in the confectioners' sugar and continue beating until mixture is smooth and of spreading consistency.

Frosts 13x9-inch cake

SALMON CAKES

"a hurry-up supper idea with good nutrition"

1 (7½ oz.) can salmon, drained and flaked
⅓ cup saltine cracker crumbs
1 slightly beaten egg
2 tbsp. chopped onion
2 tbsp. milk
1 tbsp. lemon juice
2 tbsp. butter or margarine

Combine all ingredients except butter, blending well. Shape into 4 flat patties. Melt butter or margarine in small skillet; sauté patties on both sides until golden brown and heated through. Add more butter to skillet, if necessary. Serve topped with White Sauce and Peas.

Serves: 2-4

WHITE SAUCE AND PEAS

2 tbsp. butter or margarine
1½ tbsp. flour
½ tsp. salt
1 cup milk
1 (10 oz.) pkg. frozen peas, cooked and drained or 1 cup canned peas, drained

Melt butter in saucepan; blend in flour and salt. Add milk; stir and cook until thick and bubbly. Add peas to hot mixture; heat through.

Makes 2 cups

CRISP-TART COLE SLAW

"salad is made ahead with an oil and vinegar dressing . . . store covered in the refrigerator . . . will stay crisp for several days"

1 large cabbage, shredded
1 medium onion, chopped
1 green pepper, finely
  chopped
1 tbsp. salt
1 cup boiling water
1 cup sugar
1 cup white vinegar
½ cup oil
1 tbsp. celery seed
1 tsp. mustard seed
1 (2 oz.) jar pimento,
  finely chopped

Combine shredded cabbage, onion and green pepper in large bowl. Sprinkle salt over top and pour boiling water over all; let stand at room temperature 1 hour. Drain in colander. Combine sugar, vinegar, oil, celery and mustard seeds; add to cabbage mixture. Stir in chopped pimento. Cover and refrigerate.

Serves 12

FROZEN LEMON DESSERT

"refreshing frozen dessert . . . smooth and rich with tangy lemon flavor"

4 eggs, separated
⅔ cup sugar
¼ cup lemon juice
1 tbsp. grated lemon peel
⅛ tsp. salt
1 cup whipping cream, whipped
¾ cup crushed vanilla
  wafers

Beat egg yolks till very thick and light; gradually beat in sugar, beating well after each addition. Add lemon juice, lemon peel and salt; blend well. Cook in double boiler over hot water, stirring constantly, till thick. Remove from heat; cool. Beat egg whites until stiff peaks form; fold into thickened mixture. Fold in whipped cream. Spread half the crumbs in bottom of freezer tray or 10x6x1½-inch baking dish. Spoon in lemon mixture; top with reserved crumbs. Freeze till firm, several hours or overnight.

Serves: 6-8

BRISKET IN MARINADE

"when planning your menu, check with the butcher
to make sure he'll have beef brisket on hand"

3½-4½ lb. boneless beef
  brisket
¼ cup salad oil

2 pkgs. seasoned meat
  marinade
1 medium onion, sliced

Brown brisket in oil in heavy roaster or deep baking pan. Prepare meat marinade following package directions; add onion slices. Pour marinade and onions over meat; cover with lid or foil and bake at 325° for 4 hours or until tender, basting occasionally.

To serve: Slice meat across grain. Serve with marinade left in pan, adding more water if necessary. Sauce also makes a good dip for French bread slices.

Serves: 6-8

TOMATO ASPIC

"as a suggestion fill center of ring mold with cottage cheese
mixed with mayonnaise, chopped green onion and green pepper"

1 (3 oz.) pkg. lemon
  gelatin
¾ cup boiling water
1 (10¾ oz.) can tomato
  soup

2 tbsp. vinegar or lemon
  juice
1 cup chopped celery
3 tbsp. chopped
  onion

Dissolve gelatin in boiling water; add soup and vinegar or lemon juice. Stir till well blended. Chill until slightly thick but not set; add celery and onion. Pour into a 1-quart mold or 6 individual molds. Chill till firm. Unmold on salad greens.

Serves 6

BREAD PUDDING

"spicy, old-fashioned pudding . . . good either warm or cold"

2 cups day-old bread cubes
2 eggs, slightly beaten
½ cup firmly packed brown
  sugar
1 tsp. cinnamon
1 tsp. vanilla

¼ tsp. salt
2½ cups milk
½ cup chopped walnuts
½ cup raisins
2 tbsp. butter or
  margarine

Combine all ingredients, except butter, in a 1½-quart casserole; mix thoroughly. Dot with butter or margarine. Place casserole in pan filled 1-inch deep with hot water. Bake at 325° for 45 to 60 min. or until a knife inserted halfway between center and edge of dish comes out clean.

Serves: 4-6

*For a good distribution of raisins and nuts, stir pudding carefully after 20 min. of baking.

FRUIT GLACÉ BAKE

"a versatile dish that can be a meat accompaniment, dessert or pudding for a large dinner party"

1 (11 oz.) can mandarin oranges, drained

1 (13¼ oz.) can pineapple tidbits, drained

1 (1 lb.) can pear halves, undrained

1 (1 lb. 5 oz.) can cherry pie filling

1 (1 lb. 5 oz.) can apple pie filling

1 (1 lb.) can sliced peaches, drained

1 (12 oz.) pkg. pitted prunes

¼ cup butter or margarine

¼ cup orange liqueur or ⅓ cup brandy (optional)

Combine all fruits in 13x9-inch baking pan. Sprinkle with a little salt and "dot" with butter or margarine. Bake at 350° for 1 hour or until bubbly and heated through. Serve hot, warm or cold.

Serves: 12-16

To Flame: Heat orange liqueur or brandy in small saucepan; ignite and pour over top of hot fruit.

As a meat accompaniment: Serve in a bowl or chafing dish.

Dessert or Pudding: Spoon into dessert dishes; pour cream over top, if desired.

This recipe is also good to use for a brunch.

MIX AND CHILL FRUIT SALADS

"easy do-ahead salads for busy days"

Mandarin Orange Salad: "garnish with stemmed maraschino cherries"

1 (1 lb. 4 oz.) can pineapple chunks, drained
2 (11 oz.) cans mandarin oranges, drained
1 (10½ oz.) pkg. miniature marshmallows
1 (3½ oz.) can flaked coconut
1 cup sour cream

Combine drained fruit with marshmallows, coconut, and sour cream. Chill for several hours or overnight.

Serves: 6-8

Cherry Salad: "substitute other pie fillings for cherry, if desired"

1 (1 lb. 5 oz.) can cherry pie filling
1 (1 lb. 4 oz) can pineapple chunks, drained
1 cup flaked coconut
1 cup sour cream

Combine all ingredients. Serve immediately or store in refrigerator. Serve in large bowl lined with salad greens.

Serves: 6-8

TOMATO PUDDING

"a colorful addition to any meal"

½ stick butter or margarine
⅔ cup brown sugar
2 cups cubed soft bread crumbs
1 10½ oz. can of tomato puree
¼ cup water
¼ tsp. salt

Melt butter; pour over bread and toss. Heat the tomato puree, water, salt and brown sugar. Simmer 5 minutes, then pour over bread cubes. Toss. Bake in a 1½-quart covered casserole for 45 minutes.

Serves 6

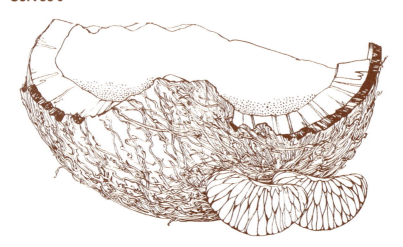

CHOCOLATE PIE

"rich chocolate filling . . . topped with meringue"

9-inch baked pie shell
1 cup sugar
¼ cup cocoa
¼ cup cornstarch
¼ tsp. salt

1½ cups boiling water
3 slightly beaten egg yolks
2 tbsp. butter or
  margarine
1 tsp. vanilla

Combine sugar, cocoa, cornstarch and salt in medium saucepan; gradually add the boiling water, blending thoroughly. Cook over medium heat, stirring constantly, until mixture thickens and boils. Cook 2 min.; remove from heat.

Add small amount of hot chocolate mixture to egg yolks; stir into chocolate mixture and cook 1 min. over medium heat. Add butter and vanilla; cool slightly. Pour into baked pie shell. Top with Meringue (page 21), spreading to edges of crust. Bake at 350° for 12-15 min. or until lightly browned.

Makes a 9-inch pie

MOLDED BEET SALAD

"delicious, colorful salad that goes well with beef and
pork roasts, as well as poultry"

1 (1 lb.) can diced beets
2 (3 oz.) pkgs. lemon
  gelatin
⅓ cup sugar
⅓ cup vinegar

1½ tbsp. mustard seed
⅛ tsp. salt
1 cup cold water
1 cup chopped celery
½ small onion, grated

Drain beets; measure liquid and add water to make 2⅓ cups. Heat liquid to boiling; remove from heat. Stir in gelatin till dissolved; add sugar, vinegar, mustard seed and salt, stirring until sugar is dissolved. Add cold water. Chill until slightly thick but not set; add celery, onion and beets. Pour into a 1½-quart mold or 12 individual molds. Chill several hours or until firm.

Serves: 10-12

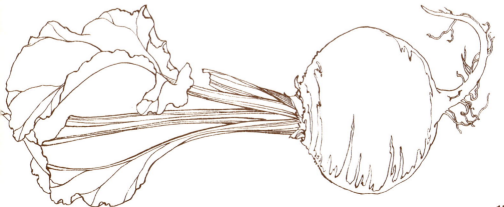

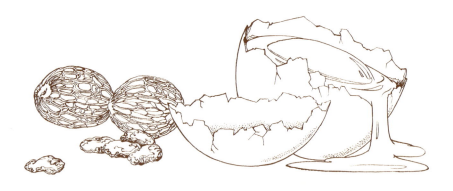

RICE PUDDING

"delicious served with cream or a fruit sauce"

2 eggs, beaten
1 cup milk
1 cup light cream
½ cup sugar

1 tsp. vanilla
1 cup cooked rice
½ cup raisins
¼ tsp. nutmeg

Combine all ingredients, except nutmeg, in a 1½-quart casserole; mix thoroughly. Place casserole in pan filled 1-inch deep with hot water. Bake at 350° for 55 to 65 min. or until knife inserted halfway comes out clean. Sprinkle nutmeg over top. Serve warm or cold.

Serves: 4-6
*For a good distribution of rice and raisins, stir pudding carefully after 30 min. of baking.

LEMON SQUARES

"rich bars with good lemon flavor . . . especially 'lemony' with lemon glaze topping"

1 cup flour
½ cup soft butter or margarine
¼ cup confectioners' sugar
2 eggs
1 cup sugar

2 tbsp. flour
½ tsp. baking powder
¼ tsp. salt
2 tbsp. lemon juice
1 tbsp. grated lemon peel

Blend flour, soft butter and confectioners' sugar thoroughly. Press evenly in 8-inch square pan. Bake at 350° for 15 to 20 min. or until lightly browned. Beat remaining ingredients together till light and fluffy. Pour over hot crust; bake an additional 25 to 30 min. or until no imprint remains when lightly touched. Cool; frost with Lemon Glaze. Cut in squares.

Makes 3 dozen squares

Lemon Glaze: Combine 1 cup confectioners' sugar, 1 tbsp. butter or margarine and 1 tbsp. lemon juice; blend until smooth and of spreading consistency. Add a few drops more lemon juice, if necessary.

Makes ⅓ cup

ORANGE SHERBET SALAD

"cool and refreshing . . . garnish with frosted grapes and serve on crispy salad greens"

2 (3 oz.) pkgs. orange
   gelatin
1 cup boiling water
1 cup orange juice

1 pint orange
   sherbet
1 (11 oz.) can mandarin
   oranges, drained

Dissolve gelatin in boiling water; add orange juice and sherbet. Beat with mixer at low speed or with hand beater until sherbet is melted and mixture is smooth. Chill until slightly thick but not set; add oranges. Pour into a 1½-quart mold or individual molds. Chill until firm.

Serves: 8-10

GERMAN POTATO SALAD

"warm, sweet-sour potato salad with flavor enhanced with bacon and onion . . . goes well with pork or ham"

5 slices bacon
¾ cup onion, chopped
2 tbsp. flour
⅔ cup cider vinegar
1⅓ cup water

¼ cup sugar
1 tsp. salt
⅛ tsp. pepper
6 cups sliced cooked
   potatoes

Fry bacon in large skillet until crisp; remove and drain. Reserve 2 to 3 tbsp. drippings. Cook and stir onion in bacon drippings until tender. Stir in flour slowly; blend well. Add vinegar and water; cook, stirring until bubbly and slightly thick. Stir in sugar, salt and pepper; simmer 10 minutes. Crumble bacon. Carefully stir bacon and potatoes into hot mixture. Heat through, stirring lightly to coat potato slices. Serve warm.

Serves: 6-8
*Salad may be made ahead, covered and refrigerated. Reheat in double boiler over hot water till thoroughly heated.

Easter Sunday

Roast Leg of Lamb or Baked Ham

*Mint Sauce *Raisin Sauce

*Creamed Potatoes & Peas   Tomato Pudding

*Pineapple-Lime Salad

*Bran Muffins

*Coconut Cream Pie   *Banana Cream Pie

Beverages

MINT SAUCE

"delicious with lamb as well as pork"

1 (10 oz.) jar red currant jelly
1 cup + 2 tbsp. chili sauce
¼ cup mint sauce

Combine red currant jelly and chili sauce in small saucepan; heat over low heat, stirring until jelly is melted and mixture is well blended. Add mint sauce; blend well and heat through.

Makes 2⅓ cups

RAISIN SAUCE

"the perfect sauce to serve with the Easter ham"

½ cup brown sugar
2 tbsp. cornstarch
1 tsp. dry mustard
2 tbsp. vinegar

2 tbsp. lemon juice
¼ tsp. grated lemon peel
1½ cups water
½ cup raisins

Combine the brown sugar, cornstarch and dry mustard in saucepan. Slowly stir in the vinegar; blend well. Add lemon juice, lemon peel, water and raisins. Stir over medium heat till thick, clear and bubbly.

Makes 2 cups

CREAMED POTATOES AND PEAS

"cook potatoes and peas ahead to save time . . . canned peas may be used, but frozen, cooked peas give a bright green color for an appetizing dish"

1 tbsp. butter or margarine
1 tbsp. flour
½ tsp. salt
1 cup milk

2½ cups cubed cooked
    new potatoes
1 (10 oz.) pkg. frozen peas,
    cooked and drained

Melt butter in medium saucepan; blend in flour and salt. Add milk; stir and cook until thick and bubbly. Add cooked potatoes and cooked peas to hot mixture; heat through. Garnish with a little chopped pimento, if desired. Pour some melted butter over the top just before serving for a richer flavor.

Serves: 4-6

PINEAPPLE-LIME SALAD

"substitute chopped celery for avocados, if desired"

1 cup crushed pineapple
1 (3 oz.) pkg. lemon gelatin
1 (3 oz.) pkg. lime gelatin

1 cup diced avocado
1 cup walnuts, chopped
Mayonnaise

Drain pineapple; reserve syrup. Add water to pineapple syrup to make 2 cups liquid. Heat to boiling; remove from heat. Stir in lemon and lime gelatin until dissolved. Add 2 cups cold water. Chill until thick but not set. Stir in fruit and nuts. Pour into a 2-quart mold. Chill until firm.

To serve: Unmold on serving dish; surround with greens. Serve with bowl of mayonnaise.
Serves: 10-12

BRAN MUFFINS

"batter can be stored covered in the refrigerator up to ten days . . . bake as needed, and serve hot, right from the oven"

1 cup boiling water
2 cups bran buds
1 cup whole bran cereal
2 cups buttermilk
1¼ cups sugar

½ cup shortening
2 eggs
3 cups flour
2½ tsp. soda
1 tsp. salt

Pour boiling water over bran cereals; mix well. Cool. Stir in buttermilk. Cream sugar and shortening in mixing bowl until light and fluffy; add eggs and beat well. Combine flour, soda and salt in bowl; blend well. Stir cooled bran mixture into creamed mixture. Add dry ingredients; stir just to moisten (batter will not be smooth).

Store in tightly covered container in refrigerator overnight or until needed. Fill well-greased muffin cups ⅔ full. Bake at 400° for 15 to 20 min. or until brown.

Makes 36 muffins

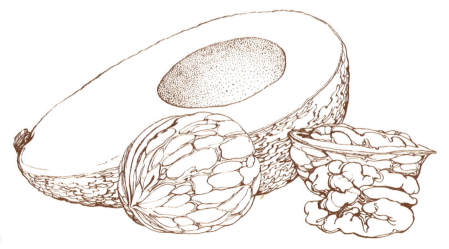

COCONUT CREAM PIE

"same recipe can be used for Banana Cream Pie (see below)"

9-inch baked pastry shell
¼ cup cornstarch
⅔ cup sugar
¼ tsp. salt
2 cups milk

3 slightly beaten egg yolks
1 cup packaged flaked
　coconut
2 tbsp. butter or margarine
1 tsp. vanilla

Combine cornstarch, sugar and salt in saucepan. Gradually add milk; blend well. Cook over medium heat, stirring constantly until thick. Blend small amount of hot mixture into egg yolks; then add to hot mixture in saucepan. Cook 1 min., stirring constantly. Add coconut, butter and vanilla; blend well. Cover and cool to lukewarm, stirring occasionally. Pour into baked pastry shell. Top with Meringue or whipped cream.

Makes a 9-inch pie

BANANA CREAM PIE

Follow recipe for Coconut Cream Pie omitting coconut. Slice 3 bananas in baked pastry shell; add filling. Top with whipped cream or Meringue.

Makes a 9-inch pie

MERINGUE FOR PIES

"whites will whip fluffier if they are at room temperature . . .
seal edges of crust with meringue to prevent 'weeping' "

3 egg whites
¼ tsp. cream of tartar

⅛ tsp. salt
6 tbsp. sugar

Beat egg whites with cream of tartar and salt in small mixing bowl at high speed of mixer till frothy. Add sugar gradually, beating well after each addition. Continue beating until sugar disappears and egg whites form stiff peaks. Top pie with meringue, spreading to edges of crust. Bake at 350° for 12 to 15 min. or until lightly browned.

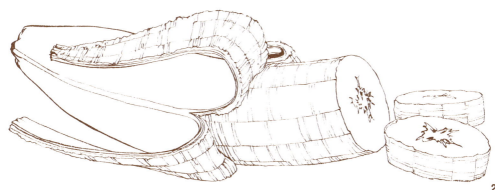

Summer

HAM LOAF

"juicy and flavorful with tangy glaze"

2½ lbs. ground smoked ham
½ lb. ground pork
2 eggs, beaten
1 cup crushed saltine crackers
¼ tsp. pepper
½ cup chopped onions
1 cup milk

Mix all ingredients thoroughly; place in ungreased 9x5x3-inch loaf pan. Bake at 350° for 2 hours. Spread Mustard Glaze over ham loaf during last half hour of baking, basting often with sauce in the pan.

Serves: 10-12

Mustard Glaze: Combine ¾ cup firmly packed brown sugar, 1½ tbsp. prepared mustard, 3 tbsp. cider vinegar and 2 tbsp. water; blend well.

HERB BREAD

"easy to prepare . . . delicious to eat"

1 loaf French bread
1 cup soft butter or margarine
2 tbsp. finely chopped green
    onion
2 tbsp. finely chopped ripe olives
2 tbsp. finely chopped parsley
1 tsp. crushed dried basil
½ tsp. crushed dried thyme
½ tsp. crushed dried
    marjoram
½ tsp. crushed dried
    tarragon

Slice French bread diagonally almost through to bottom crust. Blend soft butter with remaining ingredients; combine well. Spread cut surfaces of slices with mixture. Place on baking sheet. Heat at 350° for 15 to 20 min. Serve warm.

Makes 1 loaf

SWEDISH CREAM

"smooth, rich and creamy . . . the perfect dessert when
served with fresh, frozen or canned fruits"

1 envelope unflavored gelatin
1 cup whipping cream
1 cup sugar
1 cup sour cream
½ tsp. vanilla
Sweetened fruit

In small saucepan, sprinkle gelatin on whipping cream to soften; add sugar. Stir over low heat until gelatin and sugar are dissolved. Remove from heat and chill until mixture begins to thicken. Add sour cream and vanilla to gelatin mixture, blending well. Pour into sherbet or parfait glasses, or chill in a 3-cup mold until set. Serve topped with sweetened fruit such as strawberries or raspberries.

Serves: 4-6

BARBECUE SAUCE

"use for spare ribs, beef ribs, chicken or in meat loaf"

Sauté 1 cup chopped onion in ⅓ cup salad oil till soft.
Add:

3 tbsp. brown sugar	1 cup water
4 tsp. dry mustard	¾ cup vinegar
1 tsp. salt	3 tbsp. Worcestershire sauce
½ tsp. pepper	Few drops hot pepper sauce
3 tsp. paprika	2 cloves garlic, ground or
1½ cup catsup	dried garlic flakes

Simmer 15 minutes. Keeps indefinitely in the refrigerator.
Makes 1 quart

CORN RELISH

"a great meat accompaniment for corn lovers"

6 cups fresh sweet corn	2 tbsp. flour
(9 or 10 ears)	¼-½ tsp. turmeric
2 cups onion, chopped (2 onions)	3 cups white vinegar
2 cups cabbage, chopped	1 cup sugar
(½ head)	1 tsp. celery seed
1 medium green pepper, chopped	½ tsp. mustard seed
1 cup celery, chopped	⅛ tsp. cayenne pepper
1 (4 oz.) jar pimento, chopped	(optional)
2 tbsp. dry mustard	

Cut corn from cobs with sharp knife; combine corn with remaining vegetables in a large kettle. Mix together mustard, flour and turmeric. Add ¼ cup vinegar to mustard mixture; stir to blend well. Add mustard mixture, remaining vinegar, sugar, and spices to vegetables, mixing well. Bring vegetables to a boil; reduce heat and simmer, uncovered, 10 to 15 min. until corn is tender. Return to full rolling boil for 1 min. Ladle into hot sterilized jars, leaving ½-inch headspace. Adjust lids. Process in boiling water bath 15 min.

Makes 5 pints
*Add 1 min. to the processing time for each 1,000 ft. above sea level.

STUFFED PEPPERS

"chili powder adds special zest"

4 medium green peppers, seeded,
  with tops removed
1 medium onion (½ cup), chopped
2 tbsp. butter or margarine
1 lb. lean ground meat
1 (8 oz.) can tomato sauce

1 (8¾ oz.) can whole kernel
  corn, drained or
1 cup cooked rice
2-3 tsp. chili powder
1 tsp. salt
½-¾ cup grated sharp
  Cheddar cheese

Cook peppers in boiling salted water about 5 min.; drain well (turn peppers upside down to drain). Sauté chopped onion in butter or margarine until tender but not brown; add meat and sauté until browned; combine with remaining ingredients. Stuff peppers with meat mixture. Place in deep baking dish; add ½-inch water in bottom of baking dish. Bake at 350° for 15 min.; sprinkle tops of filled peppers with grated cheese. Continue to bake 15 min. until cheese is melted and meat is hot through.

Serves: 4

*May be made ahead of time or even the day before; if so, bake longer.

ZUCCHINI RELISH

"so good with hamburgers or pot roast"

10 cups (about 5 lbs.) zucchini,
  ground
4 large onions, ground
4 large green bell peppers, ground
4 large red bell peppers, ground
2½ cups cider vinegar

4 cups sugar
2 tbsp. corn starch
1 tsp. turmeric
1 tsp. nutmeg
2 tsp. celery seed
¼ tsp. pepper

Put the zucchini, onions and peppers through food grinder using medium blade, sprinkle with ½ cup salt. Let stand over night. In the morning, drain and rinse well with cold water. Mix together the remaining ingredients. Bring to a boil in a large kettle. Add the ground vegetables, then simmer for 30 min. Ladle into hot jars leaving ½-inch headspace.

Makes 7 pints

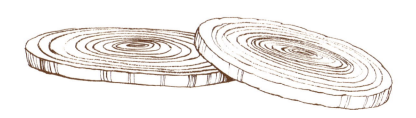

ZUCCHINI OR YELLOW SUMMER SQUASH CASSEROLE

"stuffing adds extra zest."

2 lbs. squash
¼ cup chopped onion
1 can cream of chicken soup
1 cup dairy sour cream

1 cup shredded carrots
1 (8 oz.) package seasoned
    stuffing mix
½ cup butter

Cook sliced squash and onion in boiling, slightly salted water for about 3 min. — squash must still be a little crisp. Drain. Combine chicken soup and sour cream. Stir in the shredded carrots, squash and onions; add salt to taste. Combine stuffing mix with the melted butter. Spread half the stuffing mix in the bottom of a 12x7x2-inch baking dish. Spoon vegetable mixture on top of stuffing, then sprinkle the rest of the stuffing on top of the vegetable mixture. Bake at 350° for 25 to 30 min. or until hot and bubbly.

Serves 6.

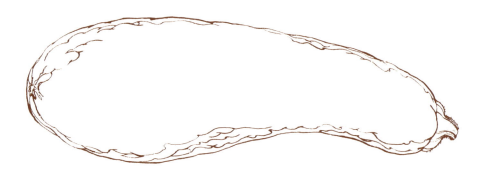

BAKED SOLE

*"an inexpensive gourmet dish . . . browned
butter adds a special flavor."*

1 lb. fillet of sole
1 egg white
1½ cups saltine cracker crumbs

1 cup butter
salt and pepper

Dry sole by patting with paper towels. Whip egg white with fork until foamy. Dip sole fillets into whipped egg white, then roll in cracker crumbs until well-coated. Place butter in shallow baking pan. Place in 400° oven until butter melts and turns golden brown (do not let butter burn). Place coated fillets in browned butter; sprinkle with salt and pepper. Bake at 400° for 30 min., basting every five minutes. At end of baking time baste all remaining butter into fish before serving.

Serves: 4

CHILI SAUCE

"adds zest to meats, baked beans and other
vegetable dishes"

12 lb. tomatoes (about 38
  medium tomatoes)
1 lb. celery (about 2 bunches),
  chopped
4 cups onion (about 4 large
  onions), chopped
3 green peppers, chopped

½ tbsp. ground
  cloves
1 tbsp. dry mustard
2 sticks cinnamon
2 lb. brown sugar
¼ cup salt
1 qt. cider vinegar

Scald tomatoes; peel. Cook in large kettle over medium heat for 15 min.; drain off half the juice. Combine remaining vegetables; add to tomatoes and simmer about 1½ hours. Tie spices in cheesecloth bag; add spices and vinegar to vegetable mixture and continue to cook 1½ hours. Remove spices; ladle mixture into hot sterilized jars. Seal, leaving ½-inch headspace. Process in boiling water bath 5 min.
Makes 6 pints

CHOW CHOW

"a tasty accompaniment to any meat, fish or poultry"

4 qts. green tomatoes
  (22 to 24)
2 qts. onions (8 or 9)
12 medium green peppers
12 ripe red peppers
4 qts. cabbage, finely shredded
  (2 large heads)

2 cups salt
2 qts. water
3 qts. white vinegar
9 cups sugar
1 cup mustard seed
¼ cup celery seed
2 tbsp. allspice

Put tomatoes, onion, green and red pepper through coarse blade of food grinder. Combine with shredded cabbage in large kettle. Dissolve salt in water; pour over vegetables and let stand overnight. Drain in colander or sieve, but do not press vegetables. Discard liquid from drained vegetables. Combine remaining ingredients; pour over vegetables. Bring to boiling; boil gently 5 min. Fill hot sterilized jars, leaving ½-inch headspace. Adjust lids. Process in boiling water bath 20 min.
Makes about 16 quarts
*Add 1 min. to the processing time for each 1,000 ft. above sea level

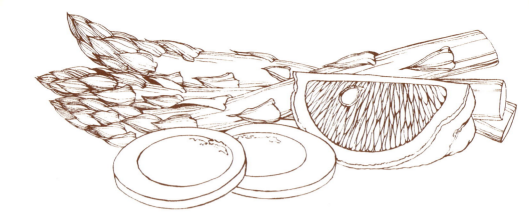

BARBECUED TROUT WRAPPED IN BACON

"bacon drippings add flavor while fish is barbecued"

4 medium trout, thoroughly   4-8 bacon slices
   defrosted, if frozen

Wash trout briefly under cold running water; pat them dry inside and out with paper towels. Wrap 1 or 2 slices bacon around fish, securing with wooden toothpicks.

Place fish on barbecue grill about 4 inches from moderately hot coals. Cook about 4 to 5 min. on each side or until flesh of trout is white and moist, and bacon becomes cooked. (Do not overcook.) When done, fish will feel firm when prodded gently with finger and will flake easily with a fork. Remove from grill to heated platter; garnish with lemon wedges or slices of tomato and sprigs of fresh parsley. Serve at once.

Serves 4

ASPARAGUS CASSEROLE

*"also good with a 1-lb. can drained asparagus or 1 lb.
cooked fresh asparagus, cut in 1-inch bias strips"*

1 (10 oz.) pkg. frozen asparagus   ⅛ tsp. pepper
3 tbsp. flour   2 cups milk
2 tbsp. butter or margarine   4 to 6 hard-cooked eggs,
1 tsp. salt   chopped

Cook asparagus as directed on package until barely tender; drain. Melt butter or margarine in small saucepan; stir in flour, salt and pepper, blending until smooth. Add milk and cook over medium heat, stirring constantly, until thickened and bubbly.

Turn half of the drained asparagus into a 1-quart casserole. Top with half the hard-cooked eggs. Pour half the sauce over eggs. Repeat with remaining asparagus, eggs and white sauce. Bake at 325° about 20 to 30 min., or until hot and bubbly.

Serves 4

PICKLED CUCUMBERS

"easy to prepare . . . needs no cooking"

4 large cucumbers (about 2½ lb.)
2 tbsp. salt
1 cup white vinegar
¼ cup sugar
½ tsp. white pepper

2 tbsp. snipped fresh
dill or 2 tsp. dried
dill weed
2 tbsp. minced parsley
(optional)

Wash cucumbers; wipe dry. Do not pare. Cut into thin slices; place in medium bowl. Sprinkle with salt; toss lightly. Cover with a plate; weigh down with a heavy can. Let stand at room temperature for 2 hours. Drain cucumber slices well; pat dry with paper towel and return to bowl.

Combine vinegar, sugar and pepper in small bowl; mix well. Pour over drained cucumbers in bowl; cover and refrigerate several hours or overnight until well chilled.

To serve: Drain cucumber slices; place in serving dish and sprinkle with dill and parsley, if desired.

Makes 6 cups

FIRE AND ICE TOMATOES

"serve as a salad or as a relish dish . . .
good accompaniment for barbecued meat or poultry"

5 large ripe tomatoes, peeled
  and quartered
1 medium green pepper,
  cut in strips
1 medium onion, thinly sliced
¾ cup cider vinegar

4½ tbsp. sugar
1½ tsp. celery seed
1½ tsp. mustard seed
½ tsp. salt
1 medium cucumber, peeled
  and thinly sliced

Combine tomatoes, green pepper and onion rings in medium bowl. In small saucepan, combine remaining ingredients except cucumber slices; bring to boil and boil 1 minute. Pour hot mixture over vegetables in bowl; let stand at room temperature until cool. Add cucumbers. Refrigerate several hours, stirring once or twice, until well chilled. Drain before serving.

Serves: 6-8

BREAD AND BUTTER PICKLES
"crunchy good . . . so easy to make"

2 cups salt
1 qt. water
3 qts. cucumbers, sliced in
  ¼-inch slices (30 to 40)
1 qt. vinegar
1 cup sugar

1 tbsp. mustard seed
1 tbsp. celery seed
½ tsp. white pepper
¼ tsp. alum
¼ tsp. turmeric

Dissolve salt in water; pour over sliced cucumbers and let stand overnight. Drain. Mix the remaining ingredients in large saucepan; bring to boiling. Pour hot mixture over cucumbers; bring cucumbers and pickling liquid to boiling. Immediately fill hot sterilized jars, leaving ½-inch headspace. Adjust lids. Process in boiling water bath 5 min.
Makes 6 to 7 pints
*Add 1 min. to processing time for each 1,000 ft. above sea level.

DILL PICKLES
"crisp and flavorful . . . select small cucumbers
for maximum number of pickles per jar"

6 qts. firm, small pickling
  cucumbers (about 30)
Ice water
12 cloves garlic, peeled and
  chopped

12 stalks dill with blossom
7 cups water
5 cups cider vinegar
1 cup salt
¼ tsp. powdered alum

Soak cucumbers in ice water overnight. Drain cucumbers; pack in 6 sterilized jars. In each jar place 2 cloves chopped garlic and 2 stalks dill with blossom. In large kettle or saucepan, combine water, vinegar, salt and alum; bring to boil. Fill jars to top with boiling liquid; seal, leaving ½-inch head space. Adjust lids. Process in boiling water bath 20 min.
Makes 6 quarts
*Add 1 min. to the processing time for each 1,000 ft. above sea level.

SPICY CHUNK PICKLES
"it took my mother fourteen days to make
pickles as good as these"

1 qt. kosher-style
  dill pickles
2 cups sugar

½ cup cider vinegar
1 tbsp. pickling spices

Drain pickles and cut into chunks. Combine sugar, vinegar and pickling spices in small saucepan; bring to a boil, stirring until sugar dissolves. Pack pickles in jar and add sugar mixture. Cover, cool and refrigerate.
Makes 1 quart

EXTRA-SPECIAL HOTDOGS

*"a children's favorite ... can be broiled in oven
or grilled over hot coals"*

Wieners
Mustard
Sweet-pickle relish

American Cheese slices, cut in
¼ inch strips
Bacon

Slit wieners lengthwise. Spread inside with mustard; add sweet-pickle relish and a strip of American cheese. Wrap each with a slice of bacon, spiral fashion, fastening each end with a wooden pick. Broil, slit side down till bacon is crisp, turn and broil till done. Serve in buns, if desired.

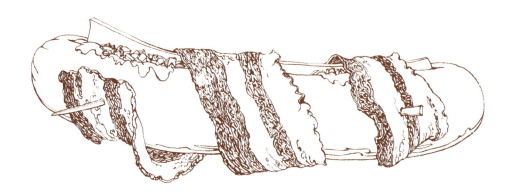

CUCUMBERS IN SOUR CREAM

*"refreshing accompaniment with fried chicken or fish ...
serve on greens for a cool summer salad"*

1 large cucumber, peeled and
  thinly sliced
¾ tsp. salt
½ cup sour cream
1 tbsp. lemon juice

½ tbsp. finely chopped
  onion
¼ tsp. sugar
⅛ tsp. white pepper
Minced parsley

Toss cucumbers with salt; cover and refrigerate until well chilled. Combine sour cream, lemon juice, onion, sugar and pepper; blend well. Reserve ¼ cup of mixture for garnish; combine cucumbers with remainder of the sour cream mixture. Refrigerate until well chilled or about 2 hours.

To serve: Arrange cucumber slices on bed of salad greens; top with small mound of reserved sour cream mixture and sprinkle with minced parsley.

Serves 4

MARINATED BEAN SALAD

"four types of beans in a delicious marinade . . .
cooked lima beans may be added also"

1 (1 lb.) can cut green beans
1 (1 lb.) can wax beans
1 (15 oz.) can garbanzo beans
1 (15 oz.) can kidney beans
½ cup chopped green pepper
½ cup chopped red onion

1 cup cider vinegar
1 cup sugar
1½ tsp. salt
½ tsp. pepper
¾ cup salad oil

Drain canned vegetables: combine with the green pepper and onion. Set aside. Combine remaining ingredients; pour over vegetables, mixing well. Cover and marinate in refrigerator overnight or 24 hours, stirring occasionally. Just before serving, drain well and serve in lettuce-lined salad bowl.

Serves: 8-10

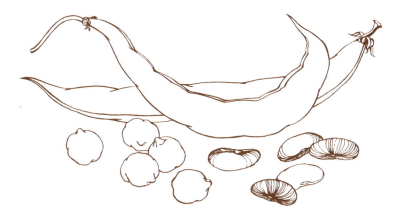

GOLDEN FRUIT NECTAR PUNCH

"a delightful beverage for graduation parties,
showers and other important occasions"

2 cups sugar
2 cups boiling water
¾ cup lemon juice
1 (12 oz.) can or 1½ cups
  apricot nectar, chilled
1 (6 oz.) can frozen limeade
  concentrate

1 (6 oz.) can frozen orange
  juice concentrate
1 (6 oz.) can frozen pineapple
  juice concentrate
2 (1 pt. 12 oz.) bottles or 7 cups
  ginger ale, chilled
1 qt. lemon sherbet

Dissolve sugar in boiling water; refrigerate until well chilled. Pour chilled mixture into chilled punch bowl; add lemon juice, apricot nectar and frozen juice concentrates. Stir until well combined; add ginger ale. Top with scoops of sherbet; garnish with fresh mint leaves, if desired.

Makes 30-35 punch cups

STRAWBERRY SHORTCAKE

"serve warm to bring out richness . . . a perfect summertime dessert"

2 cups flour
2 tbsp. sugar
1 tbsp. baking powder
½ tsp. salt
½ cup butter or margarine
1 beaten egg

⅔ cup light cream
Softened butter or margarine
3 to 4 cups sweetened, halved
  strawberries
1 cup whipping cream

Blend together flour, sugar, baking powder and salt in medium bowl; cut in the ½ cup butter or margarine till mixture resembles coarse crumbs. Combine egg and light cream; add all at once to flour mixture, stirring with fork just until moistened. Spread dough in greased 8-inch round cake pan, building up sides slightly. Bake at 450° for 15 to 18 min., or until golden brown. Remove from pan onto cooling rack; cool 5 min.

To serve: Gently slit shortcake horizontally in two layers with sharp knife, lift top off carefully. Spread softened butter or margarine over bottom layer. Whip cream to soft peaks. Spoon half the strawberries and whipped cream over bottom cake layer; top with second layer. Spoon remaining strawberries and whipped cream over top. Serve while cake is still warm.

Serves: 6-8
*On a busy day, a delicious shortcake can be made with "Lorna Doone"® cookies. Top cookies with sweetened strawberries; pour whipping cream or half and half over berries. Serve immediately.

GLAZED FRESH STRAWBERRY PIE

"luscious summer dessert . . . fresh berries covered with shiny, sweetened fruit glaze"

9-inch baked pastry shell
1½ quarts fresh strawberries,
  washed, hulled and patted dry
  with paper towel
1 cup sugar

2½ tbsp. cornstarch
½ cup water
1 tbsp. butter or margarine
Red food coloring
  (optional)

Place 1 quart fresh strawberries in cooled pastry shell. Crush remaining berries in medium saucepan; add sugar, cornstarch and water, blending well. Cook over medium heat, stirring constantly, until mixture thickens and boils; boil and stir 2 min. Add butter and few drops food coloring, if desired; stir until well blended. Strain mixture and cool. Pour cooled glaze over berries in pie shell. Chill until set, about 3 hours. Serve with sweetened whipped cream.

Serves 6

PEPPER JELLY

"good accompaniment for meat and poultry"

¼ cup hot jalapeno peppers (1-2 canned peppers), rinsed, seeded and finely chopped
¾ cup ripe red bell pepper, ground
¾ cup green bell pepper, ground
6½ cups sugar
1½ cups white vinegar
1 (6 oz.) bottle liquid pectin

Put red and green peppers through food grinder using medium blade. Drain mixture, reserving juice; add the jalapeno peppers. Combine juice from ground peppers, sugar and vinegar in large saucepan; bring to boil and remove from heat. Add peppers and liquid pectin, stirring until mixture thickens. Fill sterilized glasses; seal.

Makes 6 cups

WILTED LETTUCE SALAD

"for variety use fresh spinach in place of lettuce . . . for best flavor and texture, serve immediately after preparing"

1 head lettuce (or 2 bunches leaf lettuce)
6 slices bacon, diced
¼ cup vinegar
¼ cup water
3 tbsp. sugar
¼ tsp. salt
⅛ tsp. pepper
6 or 8 green onions, minced
2 hard cooked eggs, chopped (optional)

Wash, remove core, drain and break up lettuce into bite-size chunks (shred leaf lettuce with knife). Place in bowl. Cook bacon in skillet until crisp; remove all but about ¼ cup bacon drippings from skillet (leave fried bacon bits in skillet). Add remaining ingredients except egg; bring to boil. Pour the hot salad dressing over lettuce and toss lightly. Sprinkle with chopped cooked egg, if desired.

Serves: 6-8

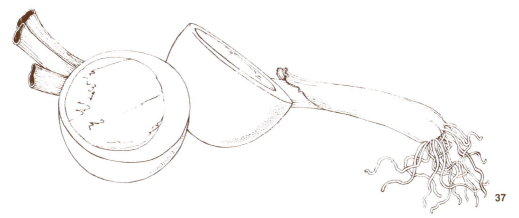

APRICOT AND LEMON SHERBET

"light, refreshing and slightly tart . . . the
perfect ending to a big dinner"

1 (3 oz.) pkg. lemon gelatin
2 cups boiling water
1 cup sugar

1 (1 lb. 1 oz.) can
  apricots
1 cup whipping cream

Dissolve gelatin in boiling water; add sugar and stir to dissolve. Cool mixture. Drain apricots, reserving 1 cup syrup. Press apricots through sieve or purée in blender. Add apricots, reserved syrup and whipping cream to cooled gelatin mixture; combine well. Pour into two freezing trays or an 8-inch square pan; freeze until nearly firm. Turn mixture into chilled bowl and beat until fluffy and smooth. (Do not let mixture melt.) Return to trays or pan and freeze until firm. Serve in sherbet or parfait glasses; garnish with sprig of fresh mint leaves, if desired.

Serves: 6-8
*This is also a perfect recipe for your ice cream freezer.

PAT'S COFFEE CAKE

"serve warm with butter . . . the perfect coffee companion . . .
also good with dinner entrée"

½ cup chopped nuts
¼ cup sugar
1 tbsp. cinnamon
1½ cups flour
1 tsp. baking powder
½ tsp. soda

½ cup butter or
  margarine
1 cup sugar
2 eggs, well beaten
1 tbsp. vanilla
1 cup sour cream

Combine chopped nuts with the ¼ cup sugar and cinnamon; set aside. Blend together the flour, baking powder and soda; set aside. Cream butter or margarine with the 1 cup sugar until light and fluffy. Add eggs and vanilla; beat well. Add dry ingredients and sour cream; beat until well blended (do not overbeat). Pour half batter into greased and lightly floured 9-inch square pan; top with half of cinnamon-nut mixture. Cover with remaining batter; top with remaining cinnamon-nut mixture. Bake at 375° for 30 to 35 min. or until golden brown.

Makes 1 coffee cake

FROZEN STRAWBERRY OR RED RASPBERRY JAM

"delicious, true fruit flavor and
color . . . needs no cooking"

2 cups crushed fresh
strawberries
4 cups sugar
½ tsp. grated lime peel

2 tbsp. lime juice
½ bottle (6 oz. size)
liquid pectin

Wash, drain, hull and crush berries; add sugar and lime peel, mixing thoroughly. Let mixture stand at room temperature 10 min. Combine lime juice with liquid pectin; stir into fruit mixture. Continue stirring for 3 min. Pour into clean containers; cover with tight-fitting lids. Let stand at room temperature 24 hours. If jam does not set, refrigerate until it does. Freeze.

Makes about 3 half pints
*Fresh peaches may be substituted for fresh strawberries, or raspberries, if desired. Remove skins before crushing fruit.

Fourth of July

* Fried Chicken or * Barbecued Hamburgers

* Potato Salad * Baked Beans

Sliced Tomatoes Cucumbers

* Homemade Vanilla Ice Cream

* Brownies

Beverages

FRIED CHICKEN
"crispy, tender and golden brown"

1 (2½-3½ lb.) broiler-fryer chicken,
  cut up
Salt

½ cup flour
¼ tsp. pepper
Salad oil and margarine

One hour or more before frying, pat chicken pieces dry with paper towel; sprinkle generously with salt and store covered in refrigerator. Combine flour and pepper; coat chicken with mixture and spread chicken pieces on rack to dry for a few minutes. Heat mixture of equal part salad oil and melted margarine (about ¼ inch) in large skillet. Add chicken and brown lightly on all sides, about 20 min. Reduce heat; cover tightly and simmer 30 to 40 min., or until tender. (Add 1-2 tbsp. water to skillet if skillet cannot be covered tightly). Turn chicken once or twice for even browning. Uncover for last 10 min. of cooking to crisp chicken.

Serves 4

*For variety chicken pieces may be dipped in milk or buttermilk before coating with flour and pepper mixture.

OVEN FRIED CHICKEN
"potato flakes make a crispy crust"

1 (2½-3½ lb.) broiler chicken,
  cut up
⅓ cup butter or margarine

2 tsp. salt
¼ tsp. pepper
⅓ cup dry mashed potato flakes

Pat chicken pieces dry with paper towel. Melt butter or margarine in 13x9-inch baking pan. Roll chicken pieces in melted butter in pan. Turn skin side up; sprinkle with salt, pepper and potato flakes. Bake at 375° uncovered about 1 hour or until tender. Do not turn during cooking.

Serves 4

BARBECUED HAMBURGERS
"grill on barbecue or broil in oven"

1½ lbs. lean ground beef
2 tsp. salt
1 tsp. "Beau Monde"®
  seasoning

¼ tsp. cracked
  pepper
2 tbsp. cream

Mix all ingredients thoroughly. Shape into 6 patties, each about 4 inches in diameter and ½-inch thick. Grill 4 to 6 inches from hot coals about 10 to 12 min., turning once, or until cooked till desired doneness. Slip hamburgers into toasted buns for serving.

To broil in oven: Broil 3 inches from heat 3 to 4 min. on each side for rare, 5 to 7 min. for medium.

Makes 6 patties

POTATO SALAD

"for firm, tender and well-shaped cubes . . . use
Russet potatoes in potato salad"

4 cups cubed cooked potatoes
  (4 medium potatoes)
1 cup chopped celery
½ cup chopped onion
¼ cup chopped sweet pickle
4 hard-cooked eggs, chopped

⅔ cup mayonnaise
2 tsp. mustard
1½ tsp. salt
3 tbsp. chopped pimento
  (optional)
2 tsp. celery seed (optional)

Combine potatoes, celery, onion, sweet pickle and hard-cooked eggs. Blend mayonnaise with mustard; stir in remaining ingredients. Mix mayonnaise mixture lightly with potato mixture until potatoes are well coated. Serve in salad bowl lined with crisp salad greens; garnish with additional hard-cooked egg slices, if desired.

Serves: 6-8

*To prevent excess moisture in salad: place freshly cooked and peeled potatoes in medium saucepan and heat over low heat until dry; cool, cube and combine with other salad ingredients.

EASY BAKED BEANS

"always a favorite at any barbecue or picnic"

4 slices bacon
½ cup chopped onion
2 (1 lb.) cans pork and beans
  in tomato sauce

4 tbsp. brown sugar
2 tsp. Worcestershire
  sauce
1 tsp. prepared mustard

Cook bacon till crisp in large skillet; drain, reserving 2 tbsp. drippings. Crumble bacon; set aside. Cook onion in reserved bacon drippings till tender but not brown. Stir in beans, bacon, and remaining ingredients; combine well. Pour into ungreased 1½-quart casserole or baking dish. Cover and bake at 375° 1 hour.

Serves: 4-6

HOMEMADE VANILLA ICE CREAM
"rich and smooth with good old-fashioned vanilla flavor"

6 medium sized eggs, beaten	¼ tsp. salt
2 cups + 6 tbsp. sugar	2¼ tbsp. vanilla
4 cups milk	3 cups whipping
2 cups half and half	cream

Prepare freezer according to manufacturer's directions. Combine eggs and sugar; beat well. Add remaining ingredients. Pour into freezer can. Freeze as directed.

Makes 1 gallon

*In most recipes the eggs and milk are cooked like a pudding, but the above recipe is the way my mother made ice cream. Once I made the pudding type, and my family refused to eat it.

BROWNIES
"chewy and moist . . . serve bars rolled in powdered sugar or with Rich Chocolate Frosting"

4 squares (4 oz.) unsweetened chocolate	4 eggs
	1 tsp. vanilla
½ cup butter or margarine	1 cup flour
	¼ tsp. salt
2 cups sugar	1 cup chopped nuts

Melt chocolate and butter or margarine in large saucepan over low heat; remove from heat. Gradually add the sugar, stirring until well blended. Add eggs, one at a time, beating well after each. Stir in remaining ingredients, beating until mixture is smooth. Spread in greased 13x9-inch baking pan. Bake at 350° for 30 to 40 min. (do not overbake). Cool slightly; cut into bars. If desired, spread with Rich Chocolate Frosting before cutting or roll in powdered sugar.

Makes about 30 bars.

RICH CHOCOLATE FROSTING
"good on cake as well as brownies"

2 squares (2 oz.) unsweetened chocolate, melted	1 egg yolk
	1½ cups confectioners'
2 tbsp. butter or margarine, melted	sugar
	¼ cup cold coffee

Combine all ingredients; stir until of spreading consistency. Add a few drops more coffee, if necessary.

Frosts 13x9-inch pan of brownies or cake.

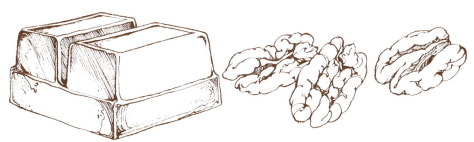

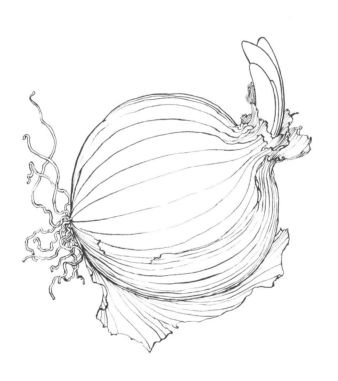

Fall

MEAT LOAF
"easy to prepare . . . zesty flavor"

1½ lb. lean ground beef
½ cup saltine cracker crumbs
    or 1 cup fine, seasoned
    bread stuffing
2 beaten eggs
1 (8 oz.) can tomato sauce
½ cup chopped onion

2 tbsp. chopped green pepper
    (optional)
2 tsp. prepared mustard
1 tsp. salt
Dash crushed dried thyme
Dash crushed dried marjoram
¼ cup chili sauce

Mix first ten ingredients thoroughly. Spread in ungreased 9x5x3-inch loaf pan. Bake at 350° for 1¼ hours. Last 15 min. of baking, spread top of meat loaf with chili sauce. After removing from pan, let stand 5 min. before slicing.
Serves 6

BAKED ACORN SQUASH
"bake with meat loaf or ham for an easy oven meal"

2 acorn squash
Salt and pepper
¼ cup butter or margarine

6 tbsp. firmly packed
    brown sugar
½ tsp. cinnamon

Cut acorn squash in half lengthwise; remove seeds. Bake cut side down in shallow pan at 350° for 35 min. or until tender. Turn cut side up; season with salt and pepper, dot with butter and sprinkle with brown sugar and cinnamon. Continue baking 20 min. longer.
Serves 4

PUMPKIN BREAD
"moist and spicy . . . spread thin slices with
softened cream cheese or butter"

⅔ cup shortening
2⅔ cups sugar
4 eggs
1 (1 lb.) can pumpkin
⅔ cup water
3⅓ cups flour
2 tsp. soda

1½ tsp. salt
½ tsp. baking powder
1 tsp. cinnamon
1 tsp. cloves
⅔ cups chopped nuts
⅔ cup raisins

Cream shortening and sugar until fluffy; stir in eggs, pumpkin and water. Mix well. Blend in dry ingredients except nuts and raisins. Add nuts and raisins; stir well. Pour into two 9x5x3-inch greased pans. Bake at 350° for 65 to 75 min. or until wooden pick inserted in center comes out clean. Remove from pans; cool on rack.
Makes 2 loaves

TWICE BAKED POTATOES

"a tasty addition to a roast beef dinner"

2 large baking potatoes
4 strips bacon, cut in fourths
¼ cup chopped green onion
2 tbsp. grated Parmesan cheese
½ cup sour cream

½ tsp. salt
½ tsp. white pepper
2 tbsp. melted butter or
   margarine
Paprika

Scrub potatoes; dry and prick with a fork. Bake at 400° for 1 hour. While potato is cooling slightly for easy handling, fry bacon in small skillet till crisp. Drain off excess drippings, leaving about 3 tbsp. in skillet. Add onion and sauté till tender but not brown; remove skillet from heat.

Cut potatoes in half lengthwise; scoop out potato insides carefully and add to skillet. Add cheese, cream and seasonings, mixing and mashing to blend thoroughly. Return skillet to low heat till mixture is heated through. Spoon mixture into potato shells; drizzle with melted butter and sprinkle with paprika. Bake at 350° for 15 to 20 min. or till lightly browned. Can be made ahead and heated just before serving time.

Serves 4

TASTY TOPPINGS FOR BAKED POTATOES

"flavor additions to make potatoes extra-special"

Sour Cream and Chives: Combine 1 cup sour cream with 2 tbsp. minced chives and ½ tsp. grated onion. Add salt and pepper to taste.

Cheese-Sour Cream Topping: Combine 2 cups grated Cheddar cheese, ½ cup softened butter, 1 cup sour cream and ¼ cup minced green onions. Add salt and pepper to taste.

Bacon Topping: Add ¼ cup crumbled crisp, cooked bacon to one of the above toppings.

Garlic Butter: Whip ½ cup soft butter with 1 tbsp. finely minced parsley and 1 clove finely minced garlic.

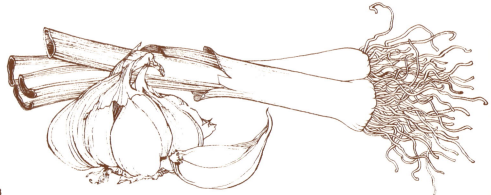

REFRIGERATED CARAMEL NUT ROLLS

"mashed potatoes make a moist, tender roll . . . rich,
buttery caramel topping with cinnamon-nut filling"

Dough:
1 pkg. active dry yeast
½ cup lukewarm water
   (105 to 115°)
⅔ cup butter or margarine
1 tsp. salt
1 cup milk, scalded

1 tsp. sugar
⅔ cup sugar
2 eggs
1 cup cold mashed potatoes
4½-5 cups flour

Caramel Coating:
⅔ cup butter or margarine
¼ cup light corn syrup

1½ cups firmly packed
   brown sugar

Filling:
½ cup firmly packed
   brown sugar
1 tsp. cinnamon

1 cup chopped nuts
¼ cup butter or margarine,
   softened

Soften yeast in warm water; stir in 1 tsp. sugar. In large mixing bowl, combine ⅔ cup sugar, butter, salt and milk; cool to lukewarm. Blend in eggs, mashed potatoes and yeast. Gradually add flour to form a stiff dough, beating well after each addition. Knead on floured surface 3 to 5 min. Place in greased bowl, turing dough to grease all sides. Cover; let rise in warm place (85 to 90°) until doubled, about 1 hour.

Punch down dough. Cover. Store in refrigerator at least 2 hours (not over 3 days). When ready to bake, prepare Caramel Coating by melting butter in a small saucepan; remove from heat. Stir in the syrup and brown sugar till well blended. Place 2 tsp. of mixture into 36 well-buttered individual muffin cups.

Combine brown sugar, cinnamon and nuts for Filling; set aside. Roll out half of dough on a lightly floured surface to an 18x12-inch rectangle. Spread with 2 tbsp. softened butter. Sprinkle dough with half of the cinnamon-nut mixture. Starting with 18-inch side, roll jelly-roll fashion. Cut into eighteen 1-inch slices; place cut side down in prepared muffin tins. Repeat procedure with other half of dough.

Cover; let rise in warm place until doubled, 1 to 1½ hours. Bake at 375° for 15 to 20 min. Invert pan immediately onto wire rack over waxed paper. Let stand 1 min. before removing pan.

Makes 36 rolls

CREAMED TUNA ON CRACKERS

"delicious served with tart Cranberry Jelly
or pickled beets"

¼ cup butter or margarine
3 tbsp. flour
½ tsp. salt
1½ cup milk

1 (6½) oz. can chunk-style
light tuna, drained
and flaked

Melt butter in saucepan over low heat. Blend in flour and salt. Stir in milk. Heat to boiling, stirring constantly. Boil and stir 1 min. Gently stir in tuna; heat through. Serve over soda crackers or toast.
Serves 4

HOT SPICED APPLE JUICE

"great drink after a football game or on Halloween"

2 qts. apple juice or cider
½ cup firmly packed brown sugar
2 whole nutmegs

4 cinnamon sticks
16 whole cloves
16 whole allspice

In large saucepan combine apple juice or cider and brown sugar. Tie spices in cheesecloth bag; crush with hammer or mallet and add to saucepan. Bring to boiling. Cover; reduce heat and simmer 15 min. Remove spice bag; discard. Ladle hot juice into mugs.
Serves 8

GRAHAM CRACKERS WITH "GOO"

"a children's favorite . . . great when Mother is too busy
to bake cookies"

2 tbsp. butter or margarine
½ tsp. vanilla
⅛ tsp. salt

1 cup confectioners' sugar
3-4 tbsp. half and half
Graham crackers

Melt butter; add remaining ingredients and blend until of spreading consistency. If necessary, thin with additional cream. Spread mixture between graham crackers.

SUSAN'S CHOCOLATE CHIP COOKIES

"a favorite with my granddaughter, Susan, as well as the whole family"

⅓ cup vegetable shortening
⅓ cup butter or margarine
½ cup granulated sugar
½ cup firmly packed brown sugar
1 egg
1 tsp. vanilla

1½ cups flour
½ tsp. soda
½ tsp. salt
½ cup chopped walnuts
1 (6 oz.) pkg. or 1 cup
    semi-sweet chocolate bits

Combine shortening, butter or margarine, sugars, egg and vanilla in large mixing bowl; beat at medium speed until mixed thoroughly. Blend together in small bowl the flour, soda and salt; add to shortening mixture. Mix well. Stir in nuts and chocolate bits. Drop dough by rounded teaspoonsful about 2 inches apart on ungreased baking sheet. Bake at 375° for 8 to 10 min., or until lightly browned but still soft. Cool on wire rack.

Makes 4 to 5 dozen

MINCEMEAT TORTE

"easy to prepare . . . serve with Tangy Lemon Sauce or whipped cream"

2½ cups fine graham
    cracker crumbs
1 tsp. baking powder
½ tsp. salt
1 cup sugar

3 beaten eggs
1 (9 oz.) pkg. mincemeat,
    broken in pieces
1 cup chopped walnuts
1 tsp. grated lemon peel

Combine crumbs, baking powder and salt; set aside. Gradually add sugar to eggs, beating until very thick; fold in crumbs, mincemeat, nuts and lemon peel. Turn mixture into a well-greased 9-inch square pan. Bake at 350° for 30 to 35 min., or till lightly browned. Cut in squares and serve warm with Tangy Lemon Sauce (page 52) or sweetened whipped cream.

Serves: 9-12

OPEN-FACED BACON, TOMATO AND CHEESE SANDWICHES

"an anytime family favorite . . . partially cook bacon, but not too crisp, before broiling"

6 slices bread
3 small tomatoes, thinly sliced
2 tsp. mayonnaise for each sandwich

6 slices American cheese
12 slices of bacon, or thin-sliced bacon, chopped and partially cooked (not crisp)

Toast bread on both sides. Place tomato slices on bread; spread with 2 tsp. mayonnaise. Salt slightly. Top with slice of American cheese and partially cooked chopped bacon bits. Broil slowly until bacon is crisp and cheese is melted. Serve at once.

Makes 6 open-faced sandwiches

GINGERBREAD

"spicy and rich . . . best served warm"

1½ cups flour
½ tsp. salt
½ tsp. baking powder
½ tsp. soda
¾ tsp. cinnamon
¾ tsp. ginger

½ tsp. allspice
½ cup shortening
½ cup boiling water
½ cup firmly packed brown sugar
½ cup dark molasses
1 egg, slightly beaten

Combine flour, salt, baking powder, soda, cinnamon, ginger and allspice in mixing bowl; set aside. Combine shortening and boiling water in large bowl; blend in brown sugar, molasses and egg. Add dry ingredients gradually; mix till thoroughly combined. Pour batter into greased 8 or 9-inch square pan. Bake at 350° for 30 to 40 min., or until wooden pick inserted in center comes out clean. Serve warm with sweetened whipped cream, spiced applesauce or Tangy Lemon Sauce.

Serves: 9-12

TANGY LEMON SAUCE

"good served warm or cold"

1 cup sugar
2½ tbsp. cornstarch
2 cups water
2 eggs yolks, beaten

½ cup lemon juice
1 tbsp. grated lemon peel
2 tbsp. butter or margarine

Combine sugar and cornstarch in saucepan; gradually add water, blending until smooth. Cook over medium heat, stirring constantly till mixture becomes thick and clear; remove from heat. Stir small amount of hot mixture into egg yolks; add to hot mixture in saucepan and cook 2 min. Add lemon juice, peel and butter; blend well. Serve warm or cold.

Makes 2¾ cups

TOMATO CHEESE RAREBIT

"substitute American cheese for Cheddar if a mild
cheese flavor is desired"

2 tbsp. butter or margarine	¾ cup canned tomatoes
2 tbsp. flour	¼ tsp. soda
½ tsp. dry mustard	1 cup shredded Cheddar cheese
⅛ tsp. pepper	2 eggs, slightly beaten
¾ cup milk	

Melt butter in medium saucepan over low heat; stir in flour and seasonings; blend well. Add milk; cook, stirring constantly till mixture is thick, smooth and bubbly. Combine tomatoes with soda; add to thickened mixture, stirring well. Add cheese, stirring till cheese melts. Stir in eggs till thoroughly combined. Serve over saltine crackers or toast.

Serves 4

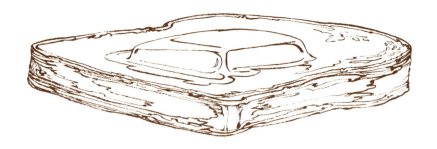

CREAMED TOMATOES

"delicious accompaniment with pork"

1 (1 lb.) can tomatoes	¼ tsp. soda
1 tbsp. butter or margarine	3 tbsp. flour
1½ tsp. sugar	¾ cup milk
¼ tsp. salt	1 slice toasted bread

Combine tomatoes, butter, sugar and salt in medium saucepan; heat over medium heat. Stir in soda. Combine flour and milk; blend well and add to hot tomato mixture. Cook, stirring constantly till mixture is thick and bubbly. Break toasted bread in small pieces and add to hot tomato mixture. Serve in sauce dish as a vegetable.

Serves 4

WHITE BREAD

"very moist . . . low in sugar"

2 pkgs. active dry yeast	1 tbsp. sugar
¼ cup warm water (105 to 115°)	1 tbsp. salt
½ tsp. sugar	4 cups milk, scalded
½ cup shortening	10-10½ cups flour

Soften yeast in warm water in small bowl; add ½ tsp. sugar. In large mixing bowl, blend shortening, sugar, salt and milk until shortening is melted; cool to lukewarm. Stir in 3 cups flour; add yeast and mix thoroughly. Mix in enough flour to make dough easy to handle.

Turn dough onto lightly floured board; knead until smooth and satiny, 5 to 10 min. Place in greased bowl, turning dough to grease all sides. Cover; let rise in warm place (85 to 90°) until light and doubled in volume, about 1 to 1½ hours.

Punch down dough; divide in four portions. Mold into balls; roll each portion into rectangle, 14x7-inches. Roll up, beginning at short side. With side of hand, press each end to seal. Fold ends under loaf. Place seam side down in greased 8½x4½x2½-inch pan; cover and let rise again in warm place until doubled, about 1 to 1½ hours.

Bake at 400° for 25 to 30 min. or until golden brown and loaves sound hollow when tapped. Remove from pans immediately; cool on wire racks.

Makes 4 loaves

*9x5x3-inch loaf pans may also be used. After punching down dough, divide into three portions.

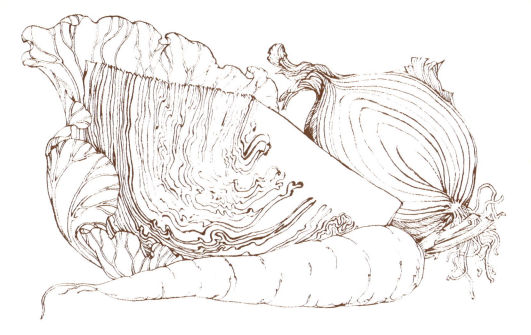

VEGETABLE BEEF SOUP

"full of meat and vegetables . . . can be a meal in itself"

2½ lb. oxtails or a good soup
    bone and some stew meat
2 tsp. salt
1 (1 lb.) can tomato wedges
2 cups cubed potatoes
1 cup shredded cabbage
½ cup chopped celery
½ cup sliced carrots
½ cup chopped onion
1½ tbsp. uncooked rice or barley
½ tsp. freshly grated pepper

Cover bones and meat with water; add salt and heat to boiling. Reduce heat; cover and simmer 3 hours. Remove bones and meat from stock; cut meat from bones into ½-inch cubes. Let stock cool slightly; skim excess fat from surface. Measure stock; add enough water so that stock plus water measures 5 cups. Strain stock into large saucepan. Add meat cubes and remaining ingredients. Heat to boiling. Cover; simmer 20 to 25 min. until carrots are tender.

Serves 6

*If using pressure cooker, cook meat for 30 min. Add enough water to make 5 cups stock, then add meat and vegetables; cook 3 min. Let the pressure return to normal.

PUMPKIN ICE CREAM

*"quick and easy . . . freeze in baked pie shell
for a spicy frozen pie"*

1 quart vanilla ice cream
1 cup canned pumpkin
¼ tsp. pumpkin pie
    spice

Soften ice cream. Stir in pumpkin and pumpkin pie spice; freeze.

Makes 1 quart

BEEF FONDUE

"allow ½ lb. meat per person"

Select tenderloin or sirloin of beef. (If less tender cuts of meat are used, sprinkle with unseasoned tenderizer). Remove all fat and tendons. Cut into 1-inch cubes. Mound the meat on platter; sprinkle lightly with salt and pepper and set out so meat will be at room temperature.

Measure the cooking oil (⅓ part clarified butter, ⅔ part oil) or all peanut oil, into fondue pot about 2 inches deep. To clarify butter, melt butter in saucepan over low heat. Let stand for a few minutes, allowing the milk solids to settle to the bottom. Skim the butter fat from the top and transfer to the fondue pot. Heat the oil and butter **on the range** until it is hot enough to brown a cube of bread. Transfer carefully to the stand on the center of the table. Light the alcohol burner or canned cooking heat.

Spear cubes of meat with fondue fork; place in hot oil and cook until meat is desired doneness. Transfer to dinner fork and dip the cooked beef in one of the Fondue Sauces (found on page 57).

*If the oil in the fondue pot is not cooking briskly, carefully return it to the range to get oil up to temperature.

APPLE CRUNCH

"crispy and fruity . . . best served warm"

6 cups pared, sliced apples (about 6 medium)	¾ cup flour
	½ cup firmly packed brown sugar
½ cup granulated sugar	¼ cup soft butter or
1 tsp. cinnamon	margarine

Place apples in greased 8-inch square pan or 1½-quart casserole. Combine sugar and cinnamon; sprinkle over apples. Combine flour, brown sugar and butter; spread mixture over sugared apples. Bake at 350° for 45 to 50 min., or until fruit is tender and top is golden brown. Serve warm with cream or ice cream.
Serves: 6-8

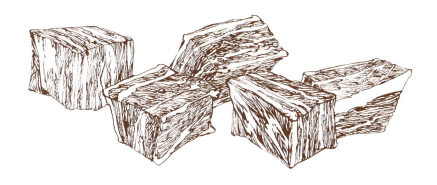

FONDUE SAUCES

"may be made ahead . . . serve 3 or 4 at a fondue dinner"

Bearnaise Sauce: "needs no cooking; serve right from blender"

4 eggs yolks	1 tbsp. chopped green onion
1 tbsp. tarragon vinegar	1 tbsp. chopped parsley
½ tsp. salt	Dash cayenne pepper
½ cup melted butter	

Place egg yolks, vinegar and salt in blender. Turn on high speed; add a little melted butter and allow it to blend. Add the remaining butter very slowly in a stream; blend until thick and well combined. Stir in remaining ingredients.

Hollandaise Sauce: Follow recipe for Bearnaise Sauce, substituting 2 tbsp. lemon juice in place of vinegar.

Sweet-Sour Sauce: Heat together ¼ cup vinegar, ½ cup pineapple juice, ½ cup brown sugar, 1 tsp. salt. Combine 1 tbsp. cornstarch and 1 tbsp. water; add to hot mixture and cook until thick and clear. Cool. Add a few chunks of pineapple, if desired.

Garlic Butter: Whip ½ cup soft butter with 1 tbsp. finely minced fresh parsley and 1 clove finely minced garlic.

Sour Cream-Horseradish Sauce: Combine 1 cup sour cream, 2 tbsp. horseradish, 1 tbsp. lemon juice, ¼ tsp. Worcestershire sauce. Salt and pepper to taste.

Tangy Mayonnaise: Combine ½ cup mayonnaise with 2 tbsp. creamy French dressing and 4 tsp. Parmesan cheese.

Thanksgiving Day

Shrimp Cocktail

*Roast Turkey with Dressing

Mashed Potatoes with Gravy *Mashed Sweet Potatoes

*Wild Rice Casserole

*Red Hot Applesauce Salad *Cranberry Jelly

*Pumpkin Pie *Apple Crumb Pie *Cocoa Pecan Pie

Beverages

THANKSGIVING TURKEY

"replace wings with large bunches of parsley when bringing the roasted turkey to the dinner table"

Amount to Serve: Allow ¾ to 1 lb. per serving when buying turkey

Remove giblets from body cavity of fresh turkey and remove wings; set aside for Rich Turkey Stock. Rinse turkey with cold water; drain and pat dry. Place Savory Turkey Dressing in neck and body cavities **just before roasting.** Do not pack tightly as stuffing must have space to expand during cooking. Fasten neck skin to back with skewer. Close body cavity with skewers and lace with string. Tie drumsticks to tail. Place on rack in a shallow open pan with breast down. Brush with melted butter; roast in 350° oven for 2 hours. Turn turkey over; cover loosely with tent of foil and continue roasting till done, allowing 20 to 25 min. per lb. or till meat thermometer reaches 185°. (Insert thermometer bulb in thickest part of the breast or center of the inner thigh muscle.) When ⅔ done, cut the cord holding drumstick and tail to insure thorough cooking. To test for doneness, press thickest part of drumstick between two fingers, protecting fingers with cloth. Meat will feel soft if done, and the leg joint will give easily when drumstick is moved up and down.

Allow turkey to stand about 15 to 20 minutes before carving. Make gravy from turkey drippings and the Rich Turkey Stock from cooked giblets and wings.

RICH TURKEY STOCK FOR GRAVY

"make day before roasting the turkey"

Roast neck, heart, gizzard and wings in shallow pan at 350° until very brown, or about 2 hours. Remove from oven; place in large pot. Cover browned giblets and wings with water; bring to boil and simmer for 2 hours. Strain stock; skim off excess fat. Add drippings from roasted turkey to stock; add enough milk to make desired amount of gravy; thicken with flour and milk for rich, brown turkey gravy.

SAVORY TURKEY DRESSING

"stuff turkey just before roasting"

Amount to Serve: Allow 1 cup stuffing per pound of ready-to-cook weight or ¾ cup stuffing per pound of dressed weight.

Prepare packaged seasoned stuffing following package directions. For variety add chopped celery, chopped onion and dried or freshly minced sage.

MASHED SWEET POTATOES

"topped with miniature marshmallows . . . . .
yams may be used in place of sweet potatoes"

¼ cup butter
½ cup milk
1 tsp. cinnamon
½ tsp. salt

6 medium-size sweet potatoes, cooked and mashed, or 1 (1 lb. 13 oz.) can sweet potatoes, mashed
2 cups miniature marshmallows

Add butter, milk, cinnamon and salt to mashed sweet potatoes. Beat till smooth, light and fluffy. Spoon into greased 1½-quart casserole. Cover with marshmallows. Bake at 350° for 20 to 30 min. or until heated through and marshmallows are lightly browned.

Serves: 6-8

WILD RICE CASSEROLE

"canned mushrooms may be used in place of fresh, if desired"

¼ cup butter or margarine
½ lb. mushrooms, sliced
1 cup wild rice

2 cups chicken broth, heated to boiling
½ cup water chestnuts, sliced
1 tsp. salt

Melt 2 tbsp. of the butter in skillet; sauté mushrooms till tender and set aside. Place wild rice in a 1½-quart casserole. Add hot chicken broth, water chestnuts, salt and remaining 2 tbsp. butter, cut in small pieces. Cover; bake at 350° for 30 min. Stir in sautéed mushrooms; cover and continue to bake 15 to 30 min. longer, or till moisture is absorbed.

Serves: 6-8

RED HOT APPLESAUCE SALAD

"good with pork and ham as well as poultry . . . for
variety, substitute chopped celery for the chopped nuts"

2½ cups boiling water
⅔ cup small red cinnamon candies
2 (3 oz.) pkgs. lemon gelatin
1 (1 lb.) can or 2 cups
   sweetened applesauce

1 (8 oz.) pkg. cream cheese
½ cup mayonnaise
½ cup nuts

Combine boiling water with cinnamon candies in saucepan; stir over
low heat to dissolve candies. Remove from heat; stir in gelatin. Blend
in applesauce. Pour half of mixture into a 2-quart mold or 8-inch
square pan; chill until firm.

Blend softened cream cheese with mayonnaise; add nuts. Spread
cheese mixture over chilled mixture. Pour remaining gelatin mixture
over cheese mixture. Chill several hours or until firm.

Serves: 9-12

CRANBERRY JELLY

"beautiful red color . . . tart, delicious flavor"

1 lb. fresh cranberries
1 cup boiling water
2 cups sugar

Place fresh cranberries in large saucepan; cover with boiling water.
Cook over medium heat, stirring constantly until berries burst and
mixture thickens (about 5 min.). Press mixture through sieve or food
mill. Add sugar; stir till dissolved. Pour into hot sterile jars, cover and
refrigerate.

Makes approximately 1 quart

*This is meant to be used as a meat accompaniment, but is also good
   on bread or rolls.

PUMPKIN PIE

"to avoid spills in the oven or splatters on crust . . .
fill pie shell at the oven"

9-inch unbaked pastry shell
2 eggs, slightly beaten
½ cup granulated sugar
½ cup firmly packed brown sugar
3½ tsp. pumpkin pie spice

1 tbsp. flour
1 (1 lb.) can pumpkin or
  2 cups cooked pumpkin
1 (13-oz.) can evaporated
  milk

Combine eggs, sugars, spice and flour. Blend in pumpkin. Gradually add milk; blend well. Turn into 9-inch pastry-lined pan. Bake at 450° for about 10 min., then at 350° for 40 to 50 min., until a knife inserted about halfway between center and outside of filling comes out clean. Cool. Serve plain or with sweetened whipped cream.

Serves: 6-8

ANNE'S APPLE CRUMB PIE

"my granddaughter Anne's favorite . . . served with whipped cream sprinkled with cinnamon and sugar"

9-inch unbaked pastry shell
6 cups pared, sliced apples
  (5 to 7 tart apples)
1 cup sugar

1 tsp. cinnamon
¾ cup flour
⅓ cup butter or margarine

Place sliced apples in unbaked pastry shell. Combine ½ cup of the sugar with cinnamon; sprinkle over apples. Combine remaining ½ cup sugar with flour; cut in butter or margarine until crumbly. Sprinkle crumb mixture over apples. Bake at 400° for 40 min. or until apples are tender. Cool.

Serves: 6-8

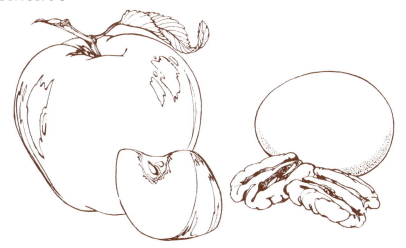

JAMES' COCOA PECAN PIE

"to serve, garnish with whipped cream mound and top with pecans . . . my grandson James' favorite"

9-inch unbaked pastry shell
1 cup sugar
⅓ cup cocoa
¼ cup flour
½ tsp. salt
3 eggs, well beaten

¾ cup dark corn syrup
¾ cup light cream
¼ cup melted butter or
  margarine
1 tsp. vanilla
1 cup pecan halves

Combine the sugar, cocoa, flour and salt in small bowl; set aside. Combine the eggs, dark corn syrup, cream, melted butter and vanilla in large mixing bowl; add the dry ingredients, stirring till smooth. Stir in pecan halves. Pour into 9-inch pastry lined pan. Bake at 325° for 60 to 70 min. until center is firm to the touch. Cool.

Serves: 6-8

Winter

SWEDISH PANCAKES

"pancakes can be made ahead . . . stack them as they are baked;
wrap in foil. Store in refrigerator and warm in 300° oven
for 15 to 20 min. before serving . . . slowly separate them
by peeling one away from the other"

3 eggs
2 cups milk
1 cup flour

1½ tsp. sugar
½ tsp. salt
¼ cup butter melted

Blend all ingredients together except butter till smooth (batter must be free from all lumps). Bring batter to room temperature; blend in melted butter. Brush a small 7 or 8-inch fry pan lightly with butter; heat over moderately high heat till small drops of water sizzle and dance on it. Immediately pour about 2 tbsp. batter into middle of pan (use small measuring cup or ladle for pouring). Quickly tilt pan in all directions to cover bottom with a thin film of batter. Cook for about a minute on one side; turn and cook about ½ min. on the other. (Final side will not brown well.) Slide pancake onto a plate; continue with the rest of the batter. For each pancake, brush pan lightly with butter.

To serve: Spread pancakes with melted butter; sprinkle with confectioners' sugar or granulated sugar and roll. Or sprinkle with sugar and spread with lingonberry preserves or cranberry jelly; roll and sprinkle with sugar, if desired.

Makes about 16 pancakes

*This batter is very good for crepes.

BUSY DAY BEEF CASSEROLE

"a spicy, hearty dish . . . so easy to put together"

1 lb. ground beef
1 medium onion, chopped
1 (1 lb.) can tomatoes
2 cups water
2 cups uncooked egg noodles
1 tbsp. chili powder
1 tsp. salt

¼ tsp. pepper
1 (8 oz.) can whole kernel
    corn, drained
1 (4 oz.) can mushrooms, drained
½ cup sliced ripe olives
    (optional)
Grated Parmesan cheese

Brown ground beef in deep heavy skillet; add onion and cook till tender but not brown. Drain off excess grease. Add tomatoes, water, noodles and seasonings; stir to moisten noodles. Cover; bring to a boil, then reduce heat and simmer 30 min., or until noodles are tender. Stir in corn, mushrooms and olives; heat thoroughly. Sprinkle with Parmesan cheese. If desired, place under broiler to brown cheese.

Serves 4-6

GUACAMOLE

''serve as a dip for crisp tortilla chips, a salad, a tortilla filling or a garnish . . . lemon juice keeps the avocados from discoloring''

6 avocados
½ cup lemon juice
1 (4 oz.) can whole green chilies, rinsed, seeded and finely chopped
1 medium onion, chopped

2-3 tbsp. mayonnaise
Salt and pepper to taste
Dash of liquid hot sauce
2 or 3 tomatoes, seeded and diced

Peel and pit the avocados; mash them with a fork while blending in lemon juice. Stir in remaining ingredients.

Makes about 4 cups

*Guacamole freezes well, but leave out the tomatoes.

To serve: Thaw; drain off excess moisture and stir in the chopped tomatoes. Chopped pimentos may be used in place of tomatoes. If you like a touch of heat, use cayenne pepper.

MONTEREY JACK CHEESE ENCHILADAS

"for variety . . . add chopped cooked chicken or
cooked ground beef to cheese filling"

3 tbsp. salad oil
2 large onions, chopped
2 large green peppers, chopped
2 (10 oz.) cans enchilada
   sauce

1 cup sour cream
12 corn tortillas
1 lb. Monterey Jack cheese, cut
   in 12 thick strips
2 cups Cheddar cheese, shredded

Heat oil in frying pan; add onion and green pepper. Sauté until
tender. Salt to taste; set aside. In a small skillet, blend the enchilada
sauce with sour cream; heat until simmering. Dip tortillas in enchilada sauce with sour cream and let stand to soften. Place part of
the onion-green pepper mixture and strip of Monterey Jack cheese
on each tortilla; roll to enclose filling. Place tortillas seam side down
in an ungreased shallow 3-quart baking dish or 13x9-inch pan. Pour
remaining sauce over all and sprinkle with shredded Cheddar
cheese. Bake uncovered at 375° for 20 to 25 min. till heated through.

Serves 6

MEXICAN CANDY

"delicious caramel candy with the consistency of fudge"

2½ cups sugar
1 cup milk
½ cup butter

1 cup chopped black
   walnuts
1 tsp. vanilla

Combine 2 cups of the sugar, milk and butter in small saucepan;
bring to a boil and remove from heat. Put the remaining ½ cup sugar
into a large heavy skillet and stir with a wooden spoon over medium
heat until the sugar is melted and caramelized to a golden brown
color. Slowly add boiled mixture to caramelized sugar stirring constantly; cook over low heat, stirring until mixture begins to boil.
Cook, stirring frequently, until it reaches the soft ball stage (240°) or
until small amount of syrup dropped into very cold water forms a soft
ball. Remove from heat. Add nuts and vanilla. Beat until mixture loses
its gloss and will hold its shape when dropped from a spoon. Pour
into a lightly buttered 8-inch square pan and cool until set. Cut into
squares before candy becomes too firm.

Makes about 36 pieces candy

ORANGE AND ONION SALAD

"good to serve with Mexican or Italian spicy food . . .
walnuts are a crunchy, tasty addition"

2 cups orange slices, white membrane removed (about 4 medium oranges)
1 cup thinly sliced mild onion rings (½ medium onion, preferably red onion)
½ cup French dressing
½ cup walnuts
1 tbsp. butter or margarine
¼ tsp. salt
7 cups crisp salad greens

Place orange and onion slices in small bowl; add French dressing and toss lightly to coat all slices with dressing. Refrigerate, covered, until well chilled, or at least 2 hours. Melt butter or margarine in small skillet; add walnuts and sauté until crisp and brown. Sprinkle nuts with salt. Just before serving place greens in salad bowl. Add orange and onion slices with the dressing; toss well. Add more French dressing, if desired. Add walnuts and toss.

Serves: 6-8

MEXICAN SALAD

"hot, spicy dressing over cold greens makes a pleasant taste sensation . . . also a great filling for crispy tacos"

1 lb. ground beef
⅓ cup chopped onion
1 (1 lb.) can kidney beans, drained
½ cup French dressing (spicy variety)
½ cup water
1 tbsp. chili powder
½ tsp. ground cumin
½ tsp. salt
4 cups shredded lettuce
½ cup sliced green onion
1½ cups shredded Cheddar cheese
1 cup tortilla chips, crumbled (If not using as a filling for tacos)

Brown meat in skillet; drain off excess grease. Add onion and cook until tender but not brown. Stir in beans, salad dressing, water and seasonings; simmer 15 min. Combine lettuce and green onions in salad bowl. Just before serving, add meat mixture and 1 cup cheese; toss lightly. Sprinkle with remaining ½ cup cheese and crisp tortilla chips. Serve immediately.

Serves: 6-8

PEANUT BRITTLE

"pull thin to make candy brittle"

2 cups sugar
1 cup light corn syrup
1 cup water
2 cups shelled unroasted
  peanuts

1 tsp. salt
2 tbsp. butter or margarine
2 tsp. soda

Combine sugar, syrup and water in a large heavy skillet. Cook slowly over medium heat, stirring constantly until sugar is dissolved. Continue cooking until mixture reaches the soft-ball stage (240°) or until small amount of mixture dropped into very cold water forms a soft ball. Add peanuts and salt; cook to the soft crack stage (290° to 300°) or until small amount of mixture dropped into very cold water separates into threads which are hard and brittle. (Mixture will be golden brown.) Watch mixture carefully to avoid burning. Remove from heat. Add butter and soda, stirring to blend (mixture will foam).

Pour onto 2 large buttered baking sheets; while still warm, pull out to desired thinness. When cold, crack into pieces.

Makes 2 pounds

CRANBERRY-ORANGE NUT BREAD

"tart, sweet and colorful . . . a welcome addition to holiday tables"

4 cups flour
1½ cups sugar
1 tbsp. baking powder
1 tsp. soda
1 tsp. salt
2 eggs, beaten

1½ cups orange juice
½ cup salad oil
2 cups cranberries, halved
1 cup chopped nuts
2 tsp. grated orange peel

Blend together the dry ingredients in mixing bowl. Combine eggs, orange juice and salad oil; add to dry ingredients, stirring until just moistened. Stir in cranberries, nuts and grated orange peel. Pour into 2 greased and lightly floured 9x5x3-inch loaf pans. Bake at 375° for 55 to 60 min., or until wooden pick inserted in center comes out clean. Remove from pan. Cool on wire rack.

Makes 2 loaves

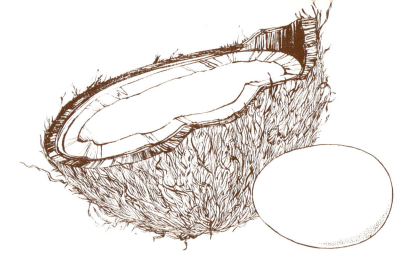

COCONUT COOKIES

"great crispy cookies . . . and a big recipe for hungry appetites"

2 cups flour
1 tsp. baking powder
1 tsp. soda
1 tsp. salt
1 cup butter or margarine
1 cup granulated sugar
1 cup firmly packed brown sugar

2 eggs
1 tsp. vanilla
3 cups quick-cooking
  rolled oats
1 cup flaked coconut
½ cup chopped nuts

Combine flour, baking powder, soda and salt in small bowl; set aside. Cream together butter or margarine and sugars until light and fluffy. Add eggs and vanilla; beat well. Blend in dry ingredients gradually; mix thoroughly. Stir in rolled oats, coconut and chopped nuts. Drop by heaping teaspoonfuls about 2 inches apart onto ungreased baking sheet. Press out with back of a fork. Bake at 350° for 10 to 15 min. until lightly browned.

Makes about 7 dozen

*This makes a very stiff dough. May want to use your hands.

FUDGE BALLS

"rich, chocolate cookies with sugar coating"

½ cup butter or margarine
1½ squares (1½ oz.)
  unsweetened chocolate
¾ cup sugar
1 egg

½ tsp. vanilla
¼ tsp. salt
2 cups flour
Confectioners' sugar

Melt butter with chocolate in saucepan over low heat; cool. Add sugar, egg, vanilla and salt; mix thoroughly. Stir in flour. Shape into balls, using a teaspoonful for each. Place on ungreased baking sheet. Bake at 375° for 8 to 10 min. or until delicately browned. While warm, roll in confectioners' sugar.

Makes about 5 dozen

JOHNNIE MUSMIE CASSEROLE

"tasty, Mexican flavor . . . a large easy-to-prepare
casserole for hearty appetites"

1 (8 oz.) pkg. egg noodles
2 lb. ground beef
2 medium onions, chopped
1 medium green pepper, chopped
2 tbsp. flour
1 (1 lb. 12 oz.) can tomatoes

2 tbsp. chili con carne
  seasoning
1 tsp. salt
¼ tsp. pepper
1 lb. shredded Longhorn
  cheese

Cook noodles as directed on package; drain. Sauté beef, onion and
green pepper in a large frying pan until beef is lightly browned and
vegetables are tender. Drain off fat; add flour and stir. Add tomatoes
and seasonings. Combine noodles with meat sauce and put in a
large flat baking dish (approximately 9x13x2-inch); top with shredded cheese. Bake at 350° for 30 to 35 min. or until heated through
and bubbly.

Serves: 8-10

*Add 1 tbsp. salad oil to boiling water when cooking the noodles. This
keeps it from boiling over.

HOLIDAY BREAD

"sweet, spicy and moist . . . baby food gives good flavor and color"

2 cups flour
1½ cups sugar
2 tsp. soda
2 tsp. salt
2 tsp. cinnamon

2 (7½ oz.) jars junior-
  sized carrots (baby food)
½ cup salad oil
4 eggs, well beaten
½ cup chopped nuts

Combine flour with sugar, soda, salt and cinnamon in mixing bowl;
blend well. Add carrots, oil, and beaten eggs; mix well. Stir in nuts.
Pour batter into 2 greased and lightly floured 8½x4½x2½-inch loaf
pans. Bake at 375° for 55 to 60 min., or until wooden pick inserted in
center comes out clean. Remove from pan; cool on wire rack.

Makes 2 loaves

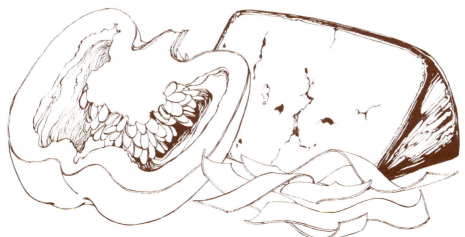

ITALIAN SPAGHETTI

"serve with crisp, green salad, crusty Italian or French bread and a dry red wine, if desired"

1½ lb. ground beef
1 medium onion, chopped
1 (1 lb.) can Italian tomatoes
1 (15 oz.) can tomato sauce
1 (12 oz.) can tomato paste
1 (10¾ oz.) can tomato soup
1 (4 oz.) can mushroom stems and pieces (with liquid)
2 tbsp. dried parsley flakes
1 tbsp. Italian seasoning
1 tbsp. oregano
1 tsp. basil leaves
1 tsp. salt
¼ tsp. minced garlic
Dash pepper
1 lb. Italian-style spaghetti, vermicelli or linguine
Grated Parmesan cheese

Cook and stir ground beef and onion in large skillet until meat is brown and onion is tender. Drain off excess fat. Stir in remaining ingredients except spaghetti and cheese. Cover; simmer 2 to 5 hours, stirring sauce occasionally. Cook spaghetti as directed on package; drain. Place drained spaghetti on platter or in large, shallow bowl. Top with sauce; sprinkle with Parmesan cheese.

Serves 8

*Sauce can be eaten after 2 hours of simmering, but has a heartier Italian flavor when simmered a longer time.

*Add 1 tbsp. salad oil to boiling water when cooking the spaghetti. This keeps it from boiling over.

GINGER COOKIES

"crisp cookies with sugared tops . . . chill
dough for easy handling"

2 cups flour
2 tsp. soda
½ tsp. salt
½ tsp. cinnamon
¼ tsp. ginger
¼ tsp. ground cloves

1 cup sugar
¾ cup shortening
1 egg
¼ cup light
    molasses
Sugar

Blend together in small bowl the flour, soda, salt and spices. In mixing bowl, add sugar to shortening; cream until light and fluffy. Add egg and molasses; beat well. Add the dry ingredients; mix well. Shape dough into balls, using a rounded teaspoonful for each; dip in sugar. Place on ungreased baking sheet, sugar side up. Bake at 375° for 10 to 12 min. or until lightly browned.

Makes about 4½ dozen

BUTTER CRESCENTS

"rich, tender cookies with crunchy pecans"

1 cup butter
5 tbsp. sugar
1 tbsp. water
1 tsp. vanilla

2 cups flour
½ tsp. salt
1 cup chopped pecans
Confectioners' sugar

Cream butter; gradually add sugar, creaming well. Add water and vanilla. Beat well. Blend in flour, salt and pecans; mix well. Chill for easier handling, if desired. Shape dough, approximately 1 tbsp. at a time, by rolling between hands into strips about 3 inches long. Curve dough in shape of crescent or half-moon. Place on ungreased baking sheet. Bake at 350° for 12-15 min. or until set but not brown. Cool; roll in confectioners' sugar.

Makes about 4 dozen cookies

"BABY RUTH"® COOKIES

"delicious cookies from the famous candy bar"

3½ cups flour
1 tsp. salt
1 tsp. soda
1½ cups sugar
1 cup butter or margarine

2 eggs
1 tsp. vanilla
6 (1.2 oz.) "Baby Ruth"® candy
    bars, cut in small pieces

Blend flour with salt and soda in small bowl. Gradually add sugar to butter in mixing bowl; cream until light and fluffy. Add eggs and vanilla; beat well. Blend in dry ingredients gradually; mix thoroughly. Stir in candy pieces. Chill dough for easy handling. Drop by tablespoonfuls onto lightly greased baking sheet. Bake at 375° for 10 to 12 min. until golden brown.

Makes about 6 dozen

PERFECT STANDING RIB ROAST
"tender, juicy meat . . . can be started in the morning
before leaving for the day"

Choose at least a 2-lb. standing rib beef roast; allow ¾ to 1 lb. per person. Anytime during the day (at least 3-4 hrs. before serving), place the room temperature roast sprinkled with salt and pepper or seasoned salts in a shallow open pan (fat side up, resting on bones or on a rack) for **exactly 45 min.** in a preheated 375° oven.

Do not add water. Do not cover. Do not baste.

Turn off oven. Leave the roast in the oven, with the door closed. Do not open oven. Turn oven on again at 375° for another 45 min. before serving. Let stand 15 min. before carving.

Note: For roasts 10 to 12 lb., leave in oven 60 min. at the beginning and 60-90 min. at the end for medium rare.

STUFFED ZUCCHINI
"zucchini may be filled ahead, covered and refrigerated . . .
top with sour cream just before baking"

6 medium zucchini	½ tsp. salt
1 (3 oz.) pkg. softened cream cheese	¼ tsp. white pepper
	1 cup sour cream
3 tbsp. onion, minced	Paprika

Place whole unpeeled zucchini in boiling water to cover; reduce heat and simmer, uncovered, till nearly tender or about 10 min. Cool slightly until they can be handled; cut each zucchini in half lengthwise and scoop out seeds into a small bowl. Combine seeds with the softened cream cheese, onion, salt and pepper.

Arrange zucchini halves in greased baking pan or dish; spoon mixture into each half. Spread the sour cream evenly over the top of each; sprinkle with paprika. Bake at 350° for 10 to 15 min. or until lightly browned and heated through. Serve immediately.

Serves: 6-8

*Cooking time of the zucchini depends upon the size. They must not be overcooked.

LEMON BREAD
"so good it can be enjoyed as a dessert bread . . .
excellent for gift-giving"

1 cup butter or margarine	1¼ cups milk
2 cups sugar	1 cup finely chopped nuts
4 eggs, separated	Grated lemon peel from 2
3¼ cups flour	lemons
2 tsp. baking powder	Fresh lemon juice from 2 lemons
1 tsp. salt	½ cup sugar

Cream butter; gradually add sugar, creaming well. Add egg yolks and beat well. Blend together the dry ingredients; add to egg-yolk mixture alternately with milk; blend just to mix. Fold in stiffly beaten egg whites, chopped nuts and lemon peel. Turn into 3 greased and lightly floured 8½x4½x2½-inch loaf pans. Bake at 350° for 55 to 60 min., or until wooden pick inserted in center comes out clean.

Combine lemon juice and remaining ½ cup sugar. Prick all over top of loaves with wooden pick. Immediately spoon lemon juice mixture over hot loaves. Cool 1 hour before removing from pans. Do not cut for 24 hours (it will slice easily).
Makes 3 loaves

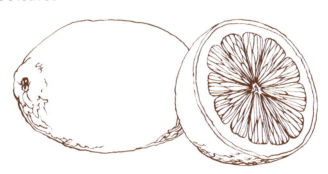

BISCUITS
"so tasty . . . with a crispy crust."

3 cups flour	1½ sticks cold butter
2½ tbsp. sugar	or margarine
4½ tsp. baking powder	¾ cup milk
¾ tsp. cream of tartar	1 egg lightly beaten
¾ tsp. salt	

Sift together in a bowl the flour, sugar, baking powder, salt and cream of tartar. With a fork, blend in the butter or margarine until the mixture resembles meal, then stir in the egg and milk. Turn dough on a lightly floured surface. Knead dough lightly once or twice and pat into a ¾-inch thick round. Cut biscuits with a 2-inch cutter. Place on a baking sheet. Bake at 400° for 15 min. or until golden.

Makes about 16 biscuits
*For altitudes of 5,000 ft. or over, use only 4 tsp. baking powder and bake at 425°.

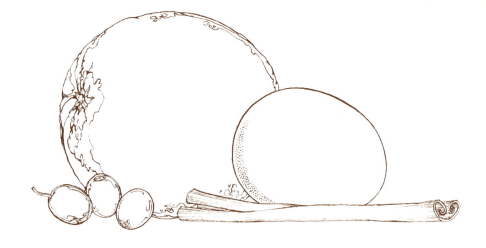

HOT CRANBERRY PUNCH

*"tangy hot punch made with fresh cranberries . . . if more
intense color is desired, add a few drops of red food coloring"*

1 lb. fresh cranberries
2 quarts water
2 tbsp. grated orange peel
6 cinnamon sticks

12 whole cloves
4 cups orange juice
1 cup lemon juice
1½ cups sugar

Combine cranberries, water, orange peel, cinnamon sticks and
cloves in large saucepan; cook until cranberries are soft. Strain. Add
orange juice, lemon juice and sugar to strained mixture; heat over
medium heat until sugar is dissolved.

Makes 16 to 20 punch cups

REFRIGERATED SUGAR COOKIES

*"rich, tender cookies made with confectioners' sugar . . .
dough roll can be stored in refrigerator, sliced
and baked when desired"*

2 cups flour
1 tsp. soda
1 tsp. cream of
  tartar
⅛ tsp. salt

1 cup butter or margarine
1¼ cups confectioners'
  sugar
1 egg
1 tsp. vanilla

Combine flour, soda, cream of tartar and salt in small bowl; set
aside. Cream butter in mixing bowl; gradually add confectioners'
sugar, creaming until light and fluffy. Add egg and vanilla; mix
thoroughly. Blend in dry ingredients; mix well. Divide dough in
half. Form each half into 2-inch round roll; wrap and chill in
refrigerator or freezer at least 4 hours, or until firm enough to slice
easily. Cut rolls into ¼-inch slices. Bake on ungreased baking
sheet at 350° for 8 to 10 min. until light brown. If you wish, sprinkle
granulated or colored sugar on top of cookies before baking.

Makes about 5 dozen

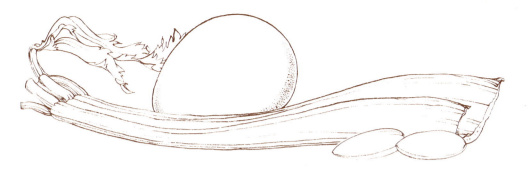

SAVORY TURKEY SCALLOP

"substitute chicken in place of turkey, if desired . . .
a good way to use up the holiday bird"

1 (8 oz.) pkg. seasoned
   stuffing
¼ cup butter or margarine
¾ cup chopped onion
¾ cup chopped celery
¾ tsp. poultry seasoning
3 cups diced cooked turkey

½ cup butter or margarine
½ cup flour
4 cups chicken broth
5 eggs
¼ cup toasted almonds
   (optional)

Prepare seasoned stuffing following package directions for moist stuffing. Melt ¼ cup butter in skillet; add onion and celery and sauté until tender. Mix with moist stuffing; stir in poultry seasoning. Spread mixture in bottom of a greased 13x9-inch baking pan or casserole. Top with turkey.

In medium saucepan, melt ½ cup butter; blend in flour, stirring till smooth. Stir in broth; heat to boiling, stirring constantly. Boil and stir 1 min. Beat eggs in mixing bowl; add small amount of hot broth, stirring constantly. Add egg mixture gradually to hot broth mixture; stir till well combined. (All this can be made ahead but do not add sauce until ready to bake.) Pour over turkey and dressing. Bake at 325° for 45 to 50 min. or until knife inserted in the center comes out clean. Last 10 min. of baking sprinkle with toasted almonds, if desired. Cut in squares. Serve with Creamy Mushroom Sauce.

Serves: 10-12

CREAMY MUSHROOM SAUCE

"a good sauce for cooked vegetables, also"

1 (10¾ oz.) can cream of
   mushroom soup
¼ cup milk

1 cup sour cream
¼ cup chopped pimento

Combine soup, milk and sour cream in saucepan. Heat, stirring until smooth and heated through; stir in pimento.

Makes 2¼ cups

BEEF-BEAN ENCHILADAS

*"can be made the day ahead, covered and refrigerated . . .
bake 45 min. when taken directly from the refrigerator"*

1½ lb. ground beef
1 medium onion, chopped
1 (1 lb.) can refried beans
1 tsp. salt
⅛ tsp. garlic powder
⅓ cup canned or bottled
   taco sauce

1 cup pitted ripe olives,
   quartered
2 (10 oz.) cans enchilada
   sauce
Salad oil for frying tortillas
12 corn tortillas
3 cups Cheddar cheese, shredded

Crumble ground beef in a frying pan; add onions. Sauté until meat is browned and onions are tender. Drain off excess grease. Stir in beans, salt, garlic powder, taco sauce and olives; heat until bubbly. Heat enchilada sauce; pour half the sauce into an ungreased shallow 3-quart baking dish.

In a small frying pan, heat the salad oil about ¼-inch deep. Dip tortillas, one at a time, in hot oil to soften; drain quickly. Place about ⅓ cup of the beef filling on each tortilla; roll to enclose filling. Place seam side down in a baking dish. Pour remaining enchilada sauce over the filled tortillas and cover with shredded cheese. Bake uncovered at 350° for 20 to 25 min. till heated thoroughly and cheese is melted.

To serve: Top each serving with sour cream combined with canned or bottled green chili salsa. Garnish with sliced pitted ripe olives.

Serves: 4-6

CHILES RELLENOS CASSEROLE

"an easy version of the popular Mexican dish . . . an excellent accompaniment to Beef-Bean Enchiladas"

2 (7 oz.) cans whole green chilies rinsed, and seeded
1½ lb. Monterey Jack cheese, grated
4 eggs, slightly beaten

½ cup milk
1 tsp. salt
½ tsp. dry mustard
¼ tsp. pepper

Line bottom of lightly greased 11¾x7½-inch baking dish or casserole with half the chilies. Sprinkle half the grated cheese over chilies; top with remaining chilies and sprinkle with remaining cheese.

Combine eggs with milk and seasonings. Pour over chilies and cheese in casserole. Bake at 350° for 30 to 35 min., or until lightly browned and set. Let cool 5 min. before cutting into squares.
Serves: 8-12

SPRITZ
"a rich, buttery pressed cookie"

1 cup butter
⅔ cup sugar
2 cups flour

3 egg yolks
1 tsp. vanilla

Cream butter and sugar until light and fluffy. Blend in remaining ingredients; mix thoroughly. Press a small amount of dough at a time through a cookie press onto an ungreased baking sheet, using the plate for the shape desired. Bake at 375° for 6 to 9 min. until set but not brown.
Makes about 5 dozen
*If desired, sprinkle with colored sugar before baking.

Christmas Eve

*Chili

Saltine Crackers   Grape Jelly

*Flan

Beverages

Christmas Day

Roast Turkey with Dressing

Mashed Potatoes with Gravy   Wild Rice Casserole

*Tossed Green Salad

*Thousand Island Dressing

*Sour Cream - Blue Cheese Dressing

*Sweet Russian Dressing   *Basic French Dressing

*Suet Pudding with Spicy Butter Sauce

*Rosettes

Beverages

CHILI

"serve with bowls of shredded Cheddar cheese, shredded lettuce,
crushed red pepper, cruets of white vinegar and catsup . . .
guests can add one or all to make the dish exactly right.
A real family favorite accompaniment is grape jelly and
saltine crackers for a delightful taste treat"

3 lb. ground beef
2 medium onions, chopped
2 cloves garlic, minced
2½ cups tomato juice
2 (8 oz.) cans tomato sauce
1 (1 lb.) can tomatoes

4 tbsp. chili con carne seasoning
1 tsp. salt
1 tsp. oregano
2 (15 oz.) cans chili beans
  in chili gravy

Cook and stir ground beef, onion and garlic in large skillet or Dutch
oven until meat is brown and onion is tender. Drain off excess fat. Stir
in remaining ingredients except beans.

Heat to boiling. Reduce heat; simmer 1 hour, stirring occasionally.
Stir in beans with gravy; continue to simmer another hour.

Serves: 6-8

FLAN

"a delicate custard baked in its own caramel sauce"

½ cup sugar
6 eggs
6 tbsp. sugar
2 cups milk

1 tsp. vanilla
½ tsp. salt
Boiling water

Place ½ cup sugar in heavy skillet; cook over medium heat until
sugar melts and forms a light brown syrup; stir to blend. Immediately pour syrup into a **warm** 8-inch round baking pan or
8¼-inch round, shallow baking dish, quickly rotating dish to cover
bottom completely. (Pan can be warmed by sitting in pan of warm
water while making caramel syrup.) Set aside.

In mixing bowl, beat eggs with 6 tbsp. of sugar. Add milk, vanilla and
salt; blend well. Pour into prepared pan or baking dish; set in shallow
pan. Pour boiling water to ½-inch level around dish. Bake at 350° for
35 to 45 min., or until sharp knife inserted in center comes out clean.
Let custard cool; refrigerate several hours or overnight.

To serve: Run small spatula around edge of dish, to loosen. Invert on
shallow serving dish; shake gently to release. The caramel acts as
sauce. Cut in wedges to serve; spoon on sauce.

Serves: 6-8

TOSSED GREEN SALAD

"for salads with taste and eye-appeal, include a combination of light and dark greens . . . crisp and tender iceberg or head lettuce, fresh spinach, romaine, endive, escarole, leaf lettuce and other variety greens"

For crisp and tender greens: Wash greens with hot water; discard stems and cores. Drain; wrap in towel and refrigerate until greens are cold and crisp. Store in a plastic bag or covered container in refrigerator.

*This sounds unusual to wash greens in hot water, but, believe it or not, it does make the greens super-crisp.

Preparing to Serve: Just before serving, break greens into bite-size portions. Combine greens in salad bowl; pour dressing over salad at the last minute to prevent wilting; toss with just enough dressing to coat the leaves lightly. If desired, add slices of raw mushrooms, raw cauliflowerettes, green peppers, onions, or cucumbers. Garnish with tomato wedges. Sprinkle salad with herbs, finely chopped fresh parsley, chives or toasted sesame seeds.

SALAD DRESSINGS

"serve tender, crisp greens and vegetables in large salad bowl
or individual bowls . . . let guests help themselves
to choice of dressing"

Sour Cream-Blue Cheese Dressing: "creamy with a mild cheese flavor"

4 oz. blue cheese
¾ cup salad oil
1 cup sour cream
¼ cup cider or wine
   vinegar

1 tsp. salt
⅛ tsp. pepper
1 clove garlic, finely minced
3 drops liquid hot sauce

Soften blue cheese at room temperature; place in small mixing bowl. With mixer at low speed, gradually add ¼ cup salad oil; beat until smooth. Add remaining salad oil and all other ingredients, one at a time; beat well after each addition until thoroughly combined. Chill.

Makes 2½ cups

Thousand Island Dressing: "zesty flavor"

¾ cup mayonnaise
3 tbsp. cream
2 tbsp. chopped green pepper
2 tbsp. chopped pimento
2 tbsp. catsup

1 tbsp. grated onion
1 tsp. Worcestershire sauce
½ tsp. salt
¼ tsp. paprika
1 hard-cooked egg, chopped

Combine all ingredients; mix thoroughly. Chill.

Makes 1½ cups

Sweet Russian Dressing: "hint of tartness with a touch of sweet"

¼ cup cider or wine
   vinegar
6 tbsp. sugar
⅓ cup catsup

2 tbsp. grated onion
1 tsp. Worcestershire sauce
Dash of cloves
1 cup salad oil

Combine all ingredients except salad oil. Let stand 10 min. Gradually add oil, blending well. Shake all ingredients well in tightly covered jar. Refrigerate. Shake again just before serving.

*Children like this dressing because of the sweet flavor.

Makes 1¾ cups

Basic French Dressing: "makes salad greens glisten"

2 tbsp. cider or wine
   vinegar or lemon juice
6 tbsp. salad oil
¾ tsp. salt

Freshly ground black pepper
1 clove garlic, finely minced
   (optional)

Combine ingredients; mix thoroughly and chill. Shake before serving.

Makes ½ cup

SUET PUDDING

"my grandmother's recipe . . . about a hundred years old"

2½ cups flour	1 cup ground suet
1 tsp. soda	1 cup firmly packed brown sugar
1 tsp. cinnamon	1 cup buttermilk
1 tsp. cloves	1 cup raisins
½ tsp. salt	1 cup chopped nuts

Mix flour with soda, spices, salt, suet and sugar. Stir buttermilk into dry ingredients; add raisins and nuts and stir until thoroughly combined. Spoon mixture into 2 greased 1-lb. coffee cans or a 2-quart pudding mold; cover with greased aluminum foil.

Place on trivet or rack in large kettle or Dutch oven; add enough boiling water to come halfway up side of can or mold. Steam (the water in the kettle should be bubbling), kettle covered, 3 hours or until wooden pick inserted in center comes out clean.

Remove coffee cans or pudding mold from water. Let stand about 10 min. With a knife, loosen pudding around edge of can; turn out of cans. Serve warm with Spicy Butter Sauce.

Serves 12

*This keeps in the refrigerator for at least a week and freezes very well.

To heat: Put in top of double boiler and heat over boiling water.

SPICY BUTTER SAUCE

"smooth and spicy . . . serve hot"

⅔ cup sugar	½ tsp. nutmeg
1½ tbsp. cornstarch	¼ tsp. cinnamon
1 cup water	1 tsp. vanilla
¼ cup butter	

Combine sugar and cornstarch in small suacepan; stir in water. Cook over medium heat, stirring constantly, until thick and bubbly. Add butter, spices and vanilla; blend well. Serve hot.

Makes 1½ cups

ROSETTES

"light, crispy fried cookies"

2 eggs
1 cup flour
1 tbsp. sugar
¼ tsp. salt

1 cup milk
Fat for deep frying
Confectioners' sugar

Beat eggs slightly; add remaining ingredients and beat until smooth. Place rosette iron in fat while heating to 375°. Remove iron; tap excess fat from iron. Dip hot iron into batter just to top (do not let batter run over top of form); then dip into hot fat. (The batter should peal off the iron.) Fry until golden brown. Drain on absorbent paper or paper towel. Sprinkle cookies with confectioners' or granulated sugar.

Makes: 4-6 dozen

*We use rosettes for a Christmas dessert topped with whipped cream and lingonberry preserves.

HOW MUCH TO BUY

Meat	Amount to Buy per Serving
Large amount of bone (ribs)	½ to 1 lb.
Medium amount of bone (chuck roast)	⅓ to ½ lb.
Small amount of bone (steaks or roasts)	¼ to ⅓ lb.
Ground meat or boneless roasts, canned ham	¼ lb.
Luncheon meat	3-4 oz.

Poultry

Chicken	
Broiling	¾ lb.
Frying, roasting, stewing	½ lb.
Duck	1 lb.
Goose	⅔ lb.
Whole turkey	
Under 12 lb.	¾ to 1 lb.
Over 12 lb.	½ to ¾ lb.
Rolled turkey roast	⅓ lb.

Fish

Whole or round	¾ to 1 lb.
Dressed, large	½ lb.
Steaks and fillets	⅓ lb.
Canned (salmon, shrimp, tuna)	3-4 oz.

RECIPE INDEX

Vegetables

Main Dishes

Breads, Pastries and Pancakes

Pies

Desserts

Cookies and Candy

Beverages

Born and raised in Topeka, Kansas, **MIRIAM BAKER LOO** is an accomplished and creative homemaker who has been an enthusiastic cook since her youth. After graduation from Washburn University of Topeka, Kansas, she was married to Orin Loo. In addition to raising three sons, with her husband, in 1950 she founded Current, Inc., a national mail order firm located in Colorado Springs. The company has grown from a basement business whose first product lines included post-a-notes and recipe cards designed by Mr. Loo to a thriving enterprise serving millions of customers today.

A participant in many gourmet food classes, Miriam Loo has been responsible for the many recipes for notes, calendars and personal enclosures in the Current product line for several years.

Long involved in volunteer activities, Miriam Loo has received national recognition for her accomplishments in community work, church leadership and business.